YOU ARE AWESOME

AN INSPIRATIONAL AND UPLIFTING Coloring BOOK

Copyright© 2020 by Saiko Print

All rights reserved. No part of this publication may be reproduced, distributed, or transmitted in any form or by any means, including photocopying, recording, or other electronic methods.

Find us at:

Amazon.com/author/saikoprint

instagram.com/saikoprint

etsy.com/saikoprint

Or you can email us at: saikoprint@mail.com

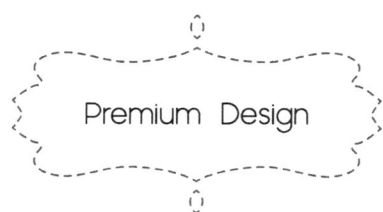

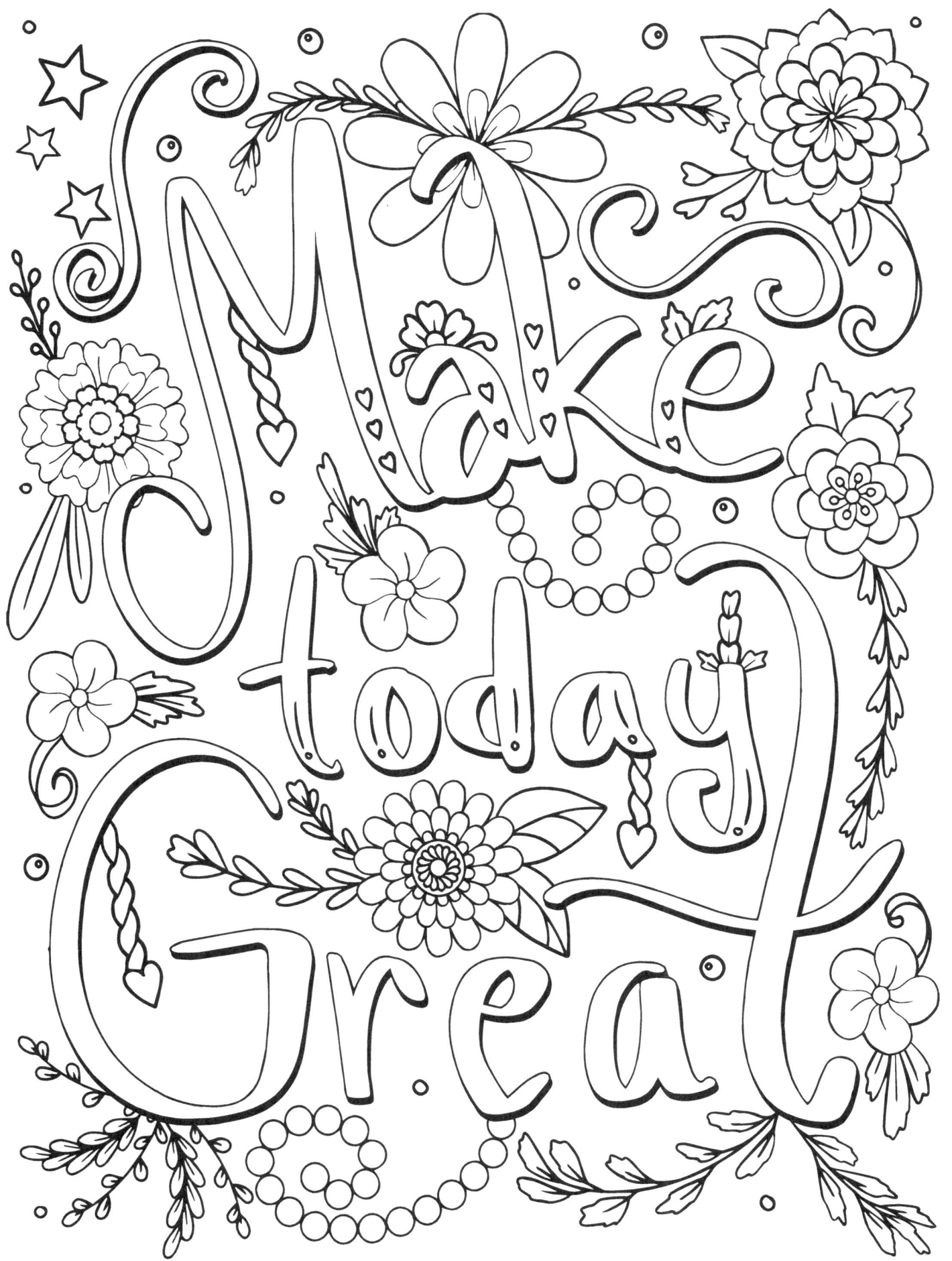

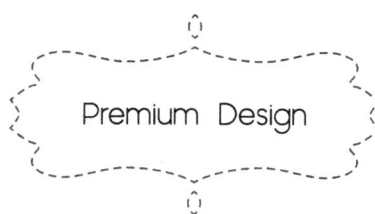

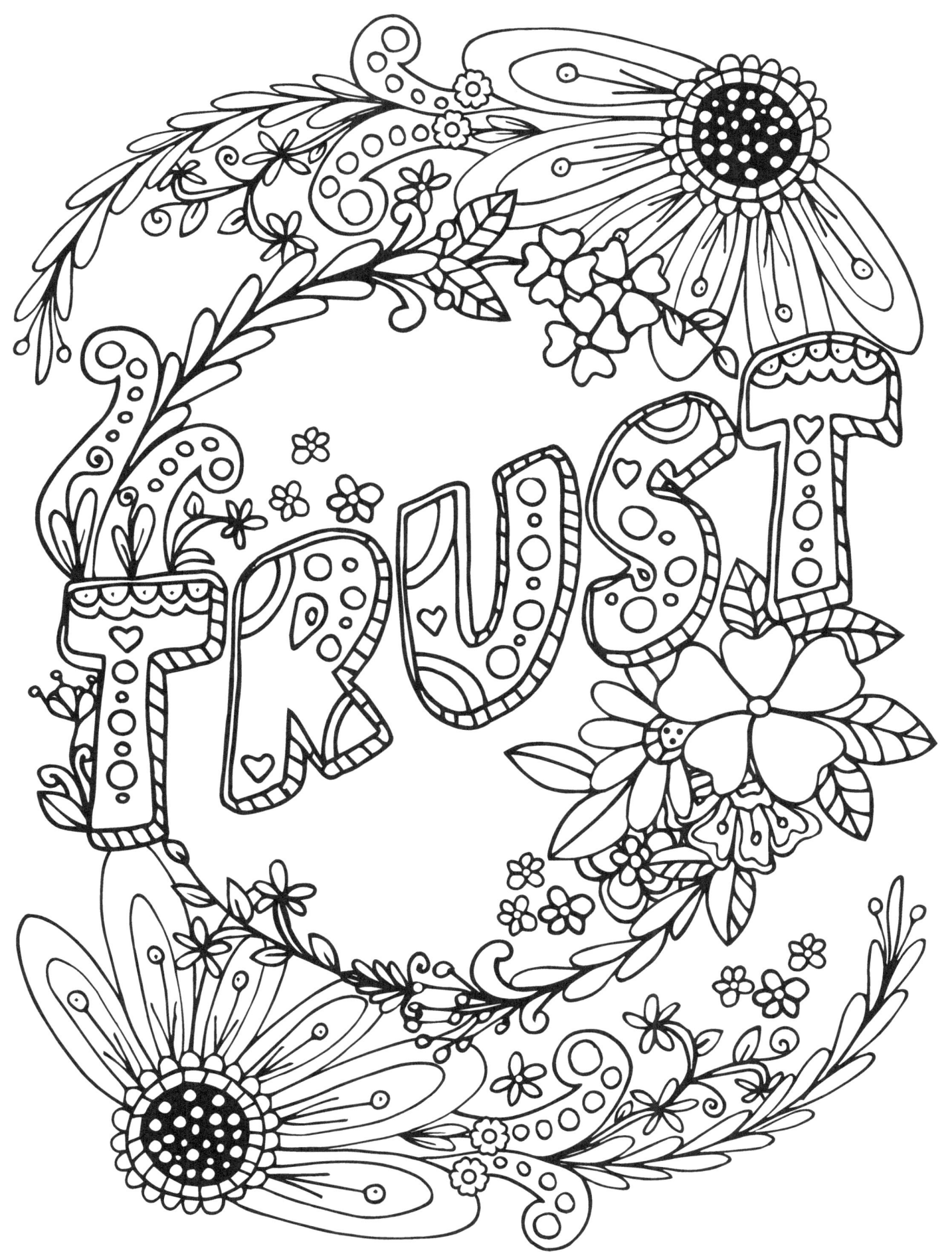

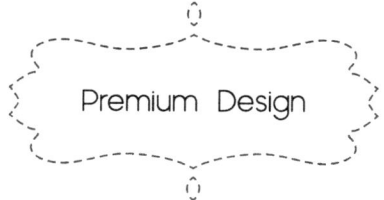

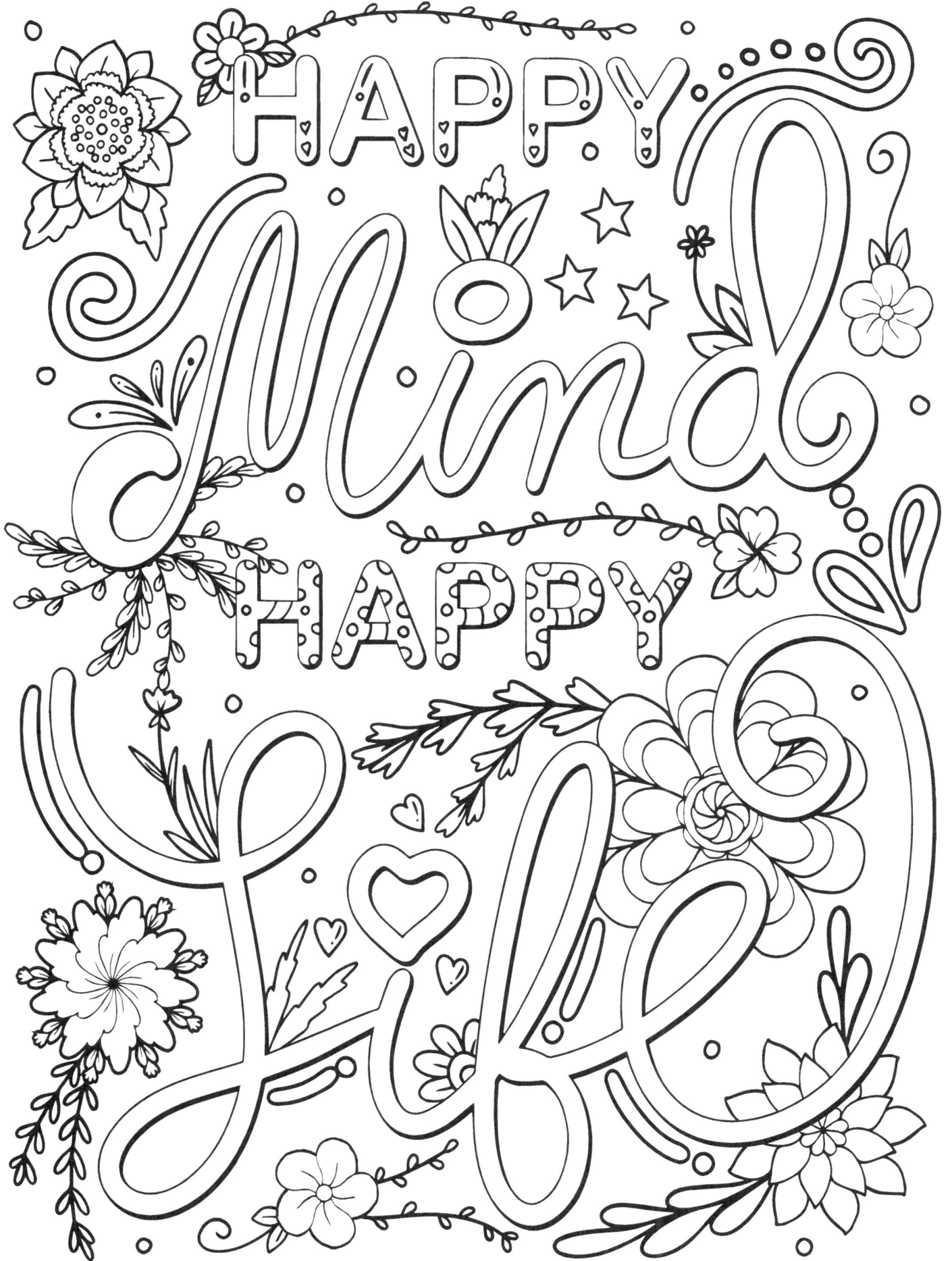

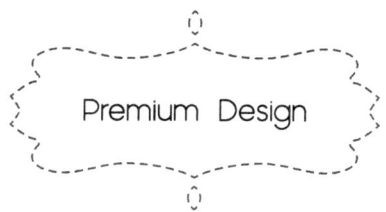

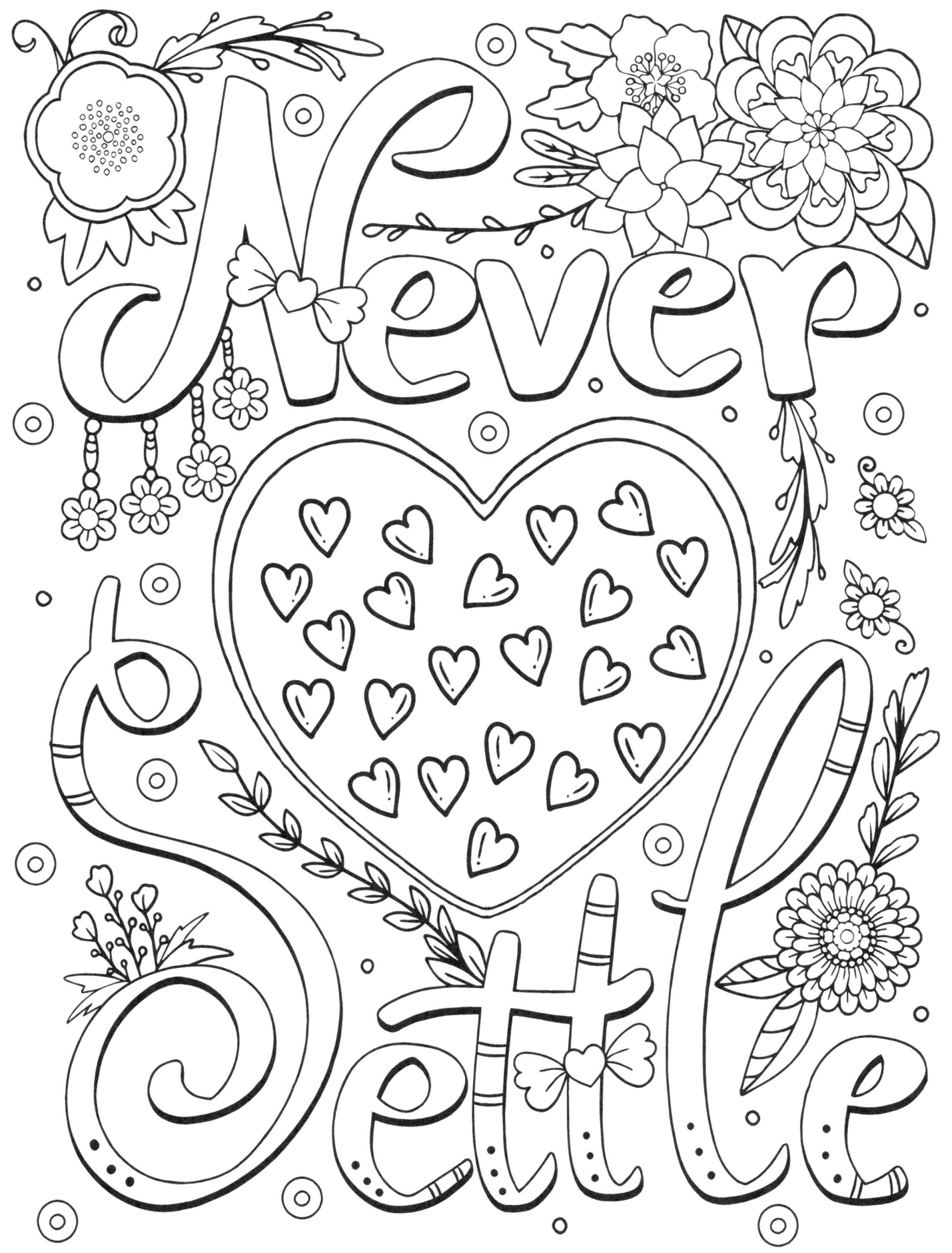

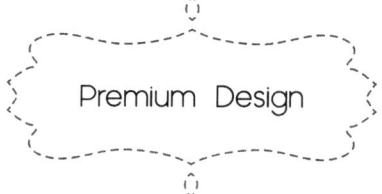

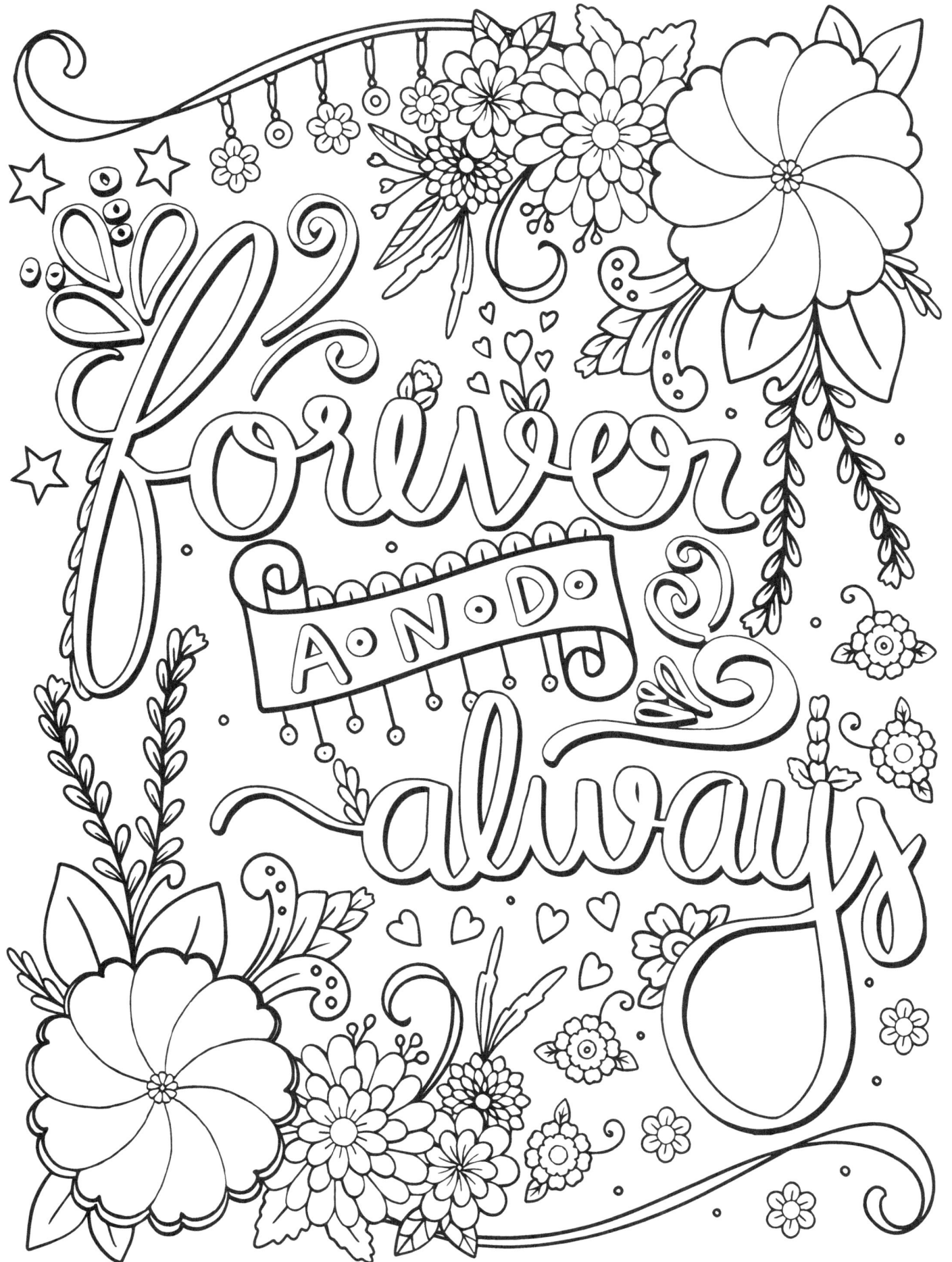

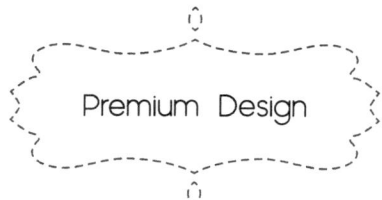

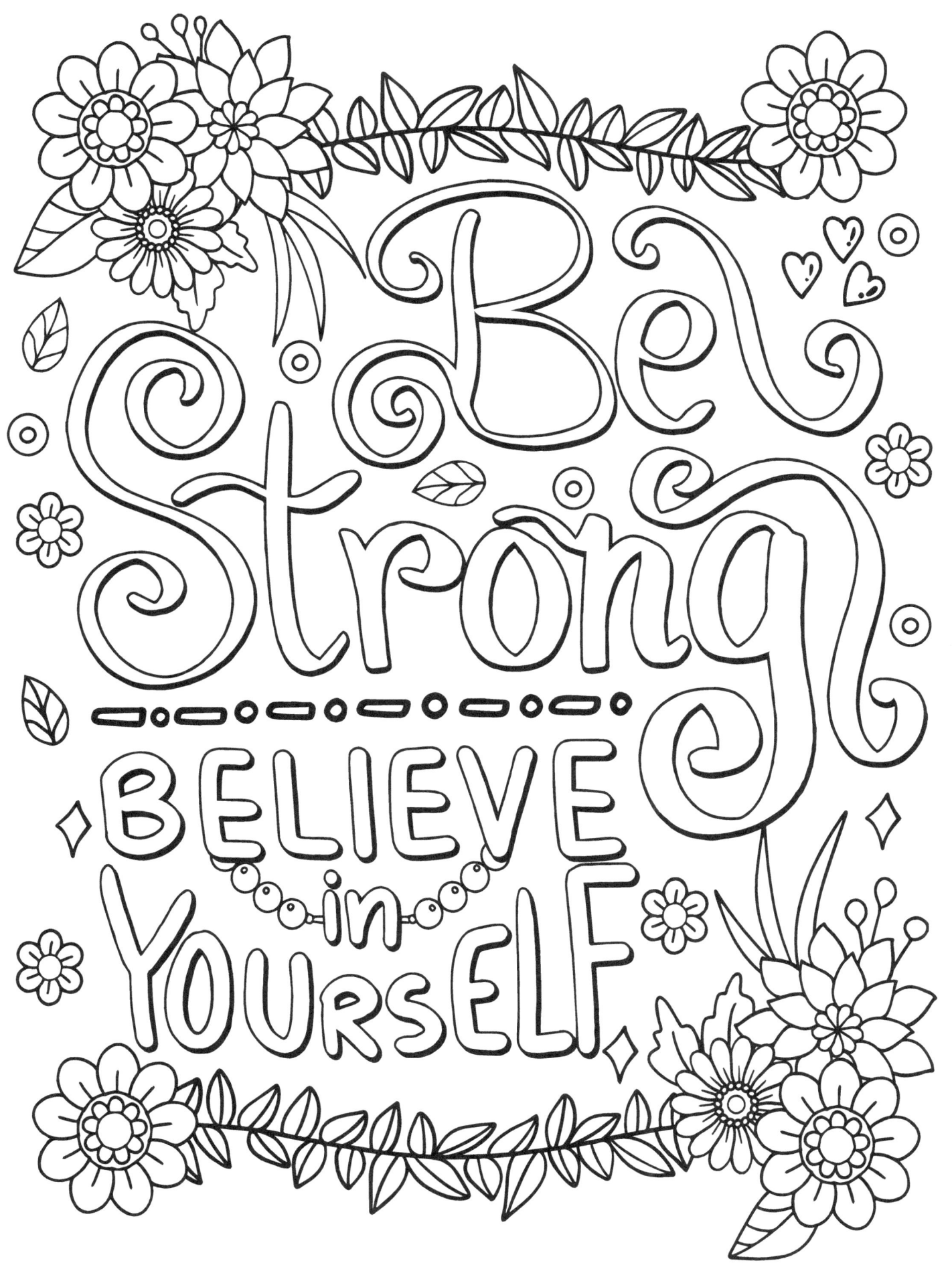

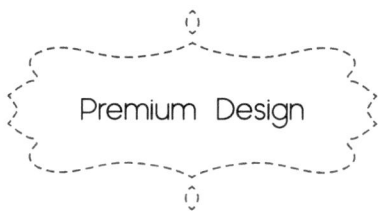

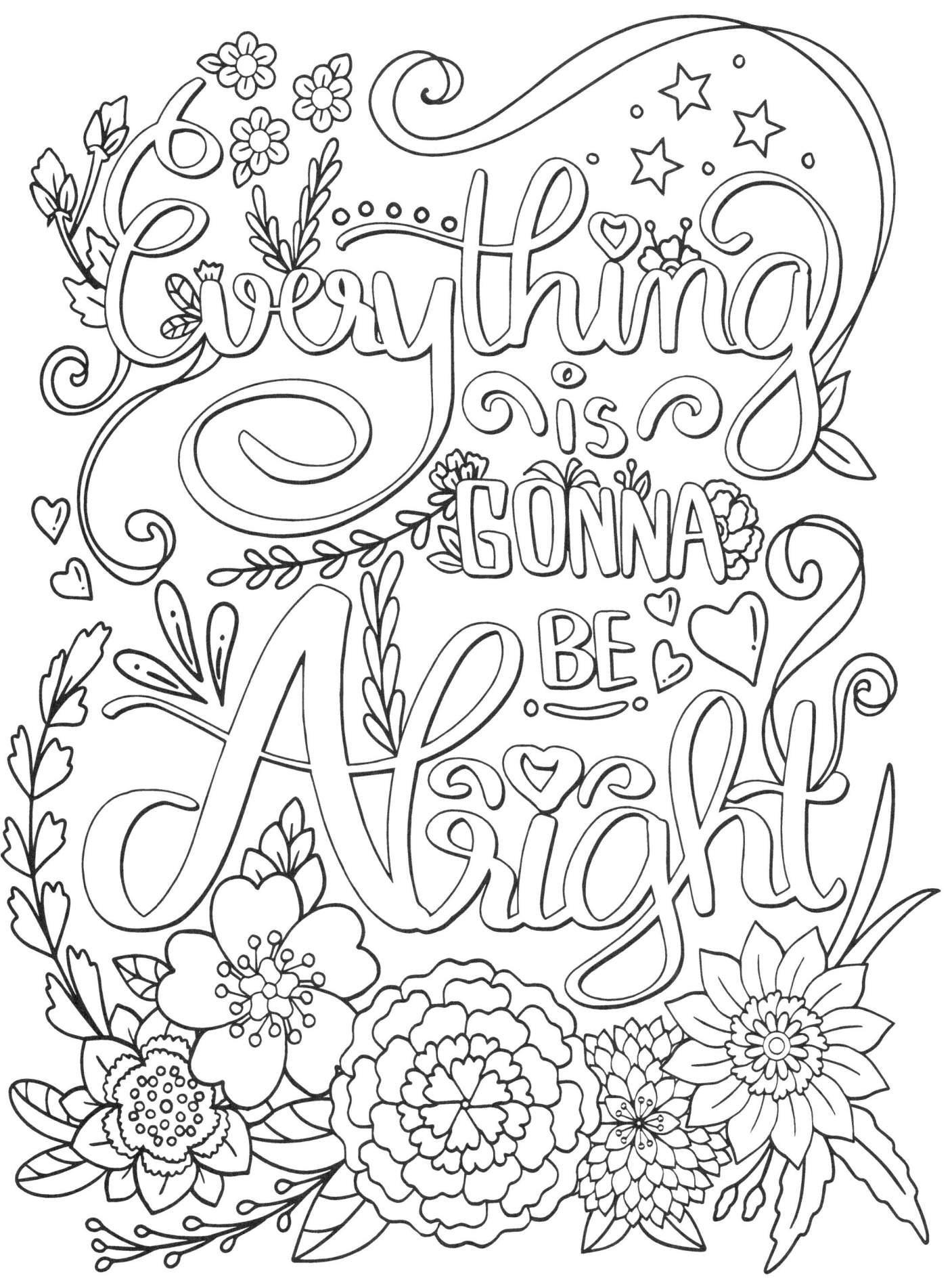

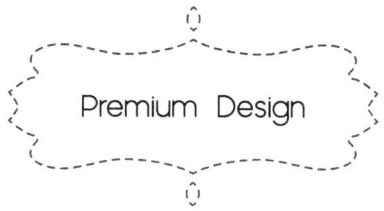

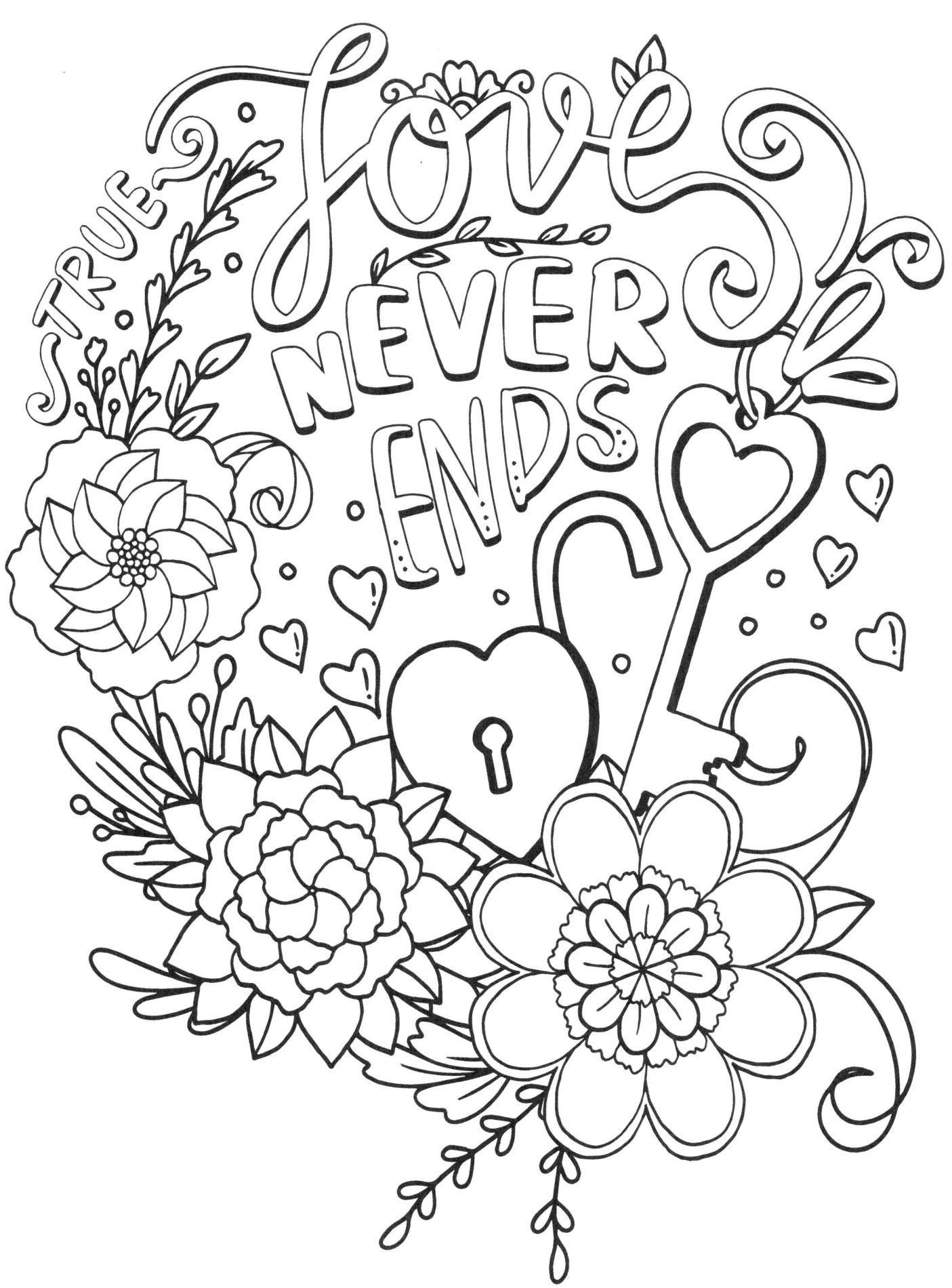

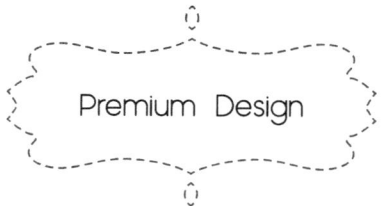

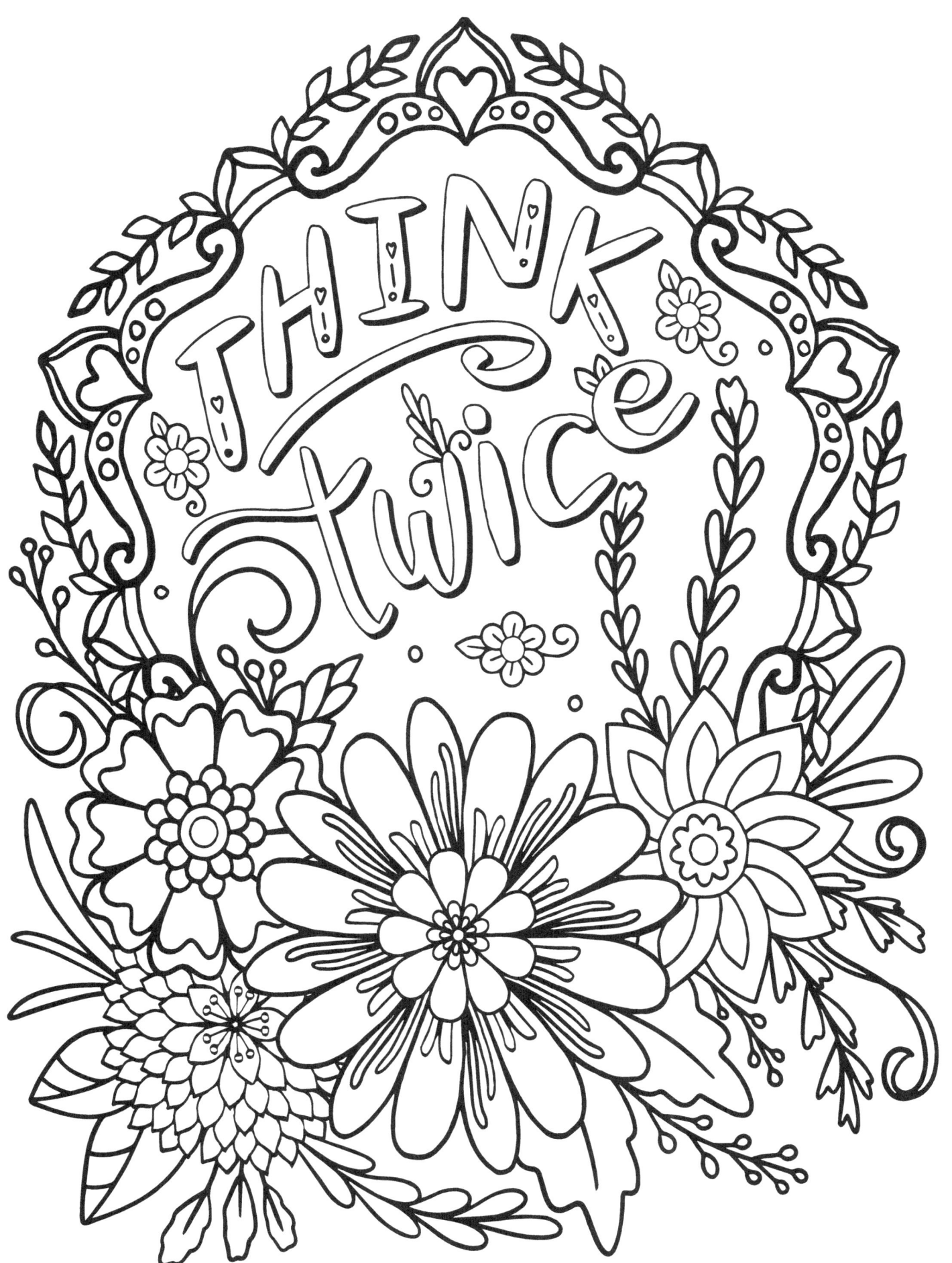

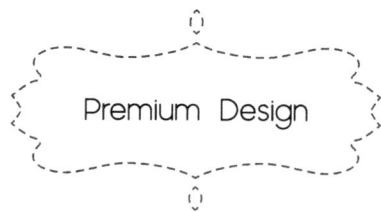

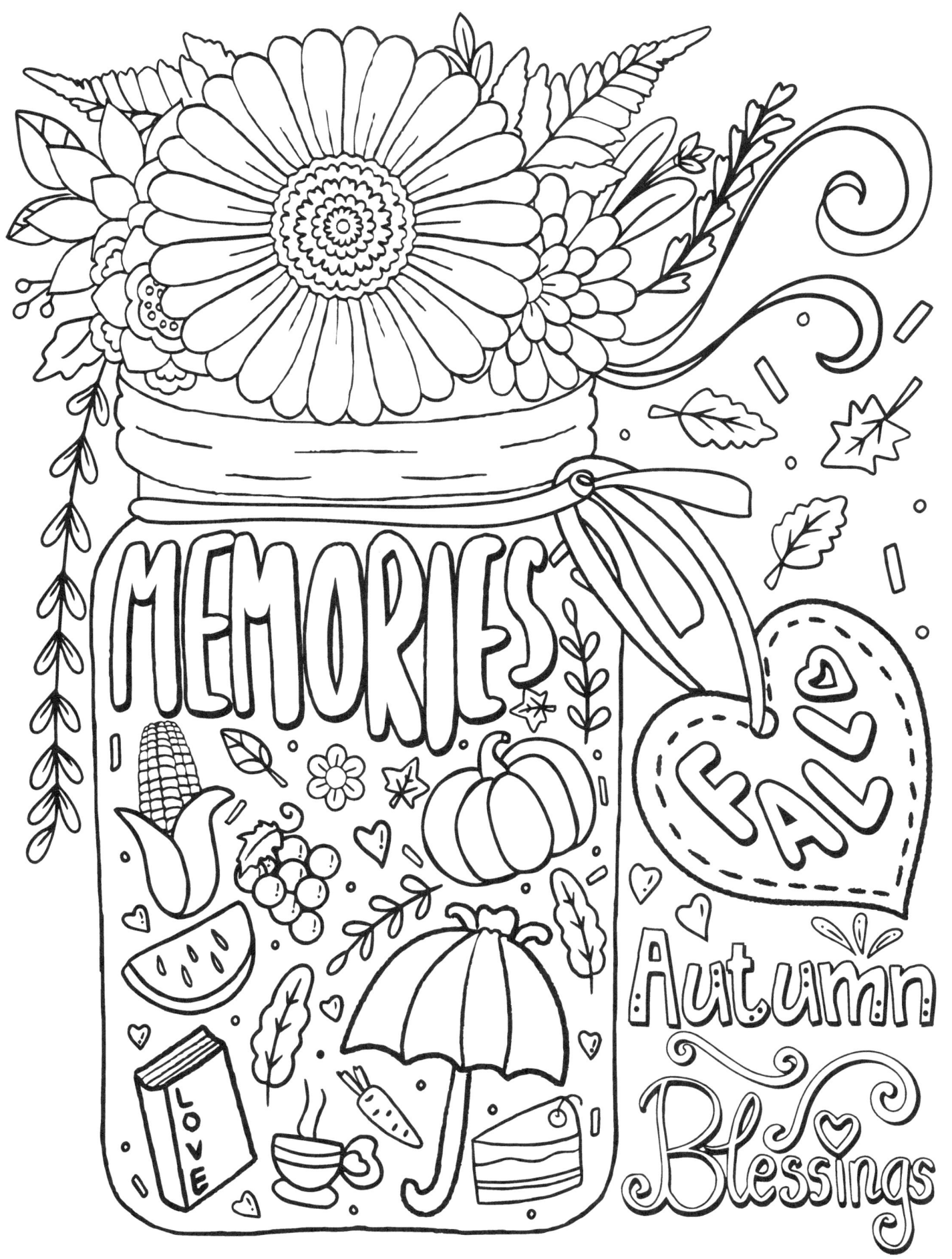

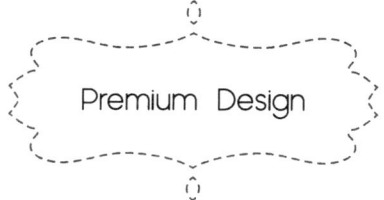

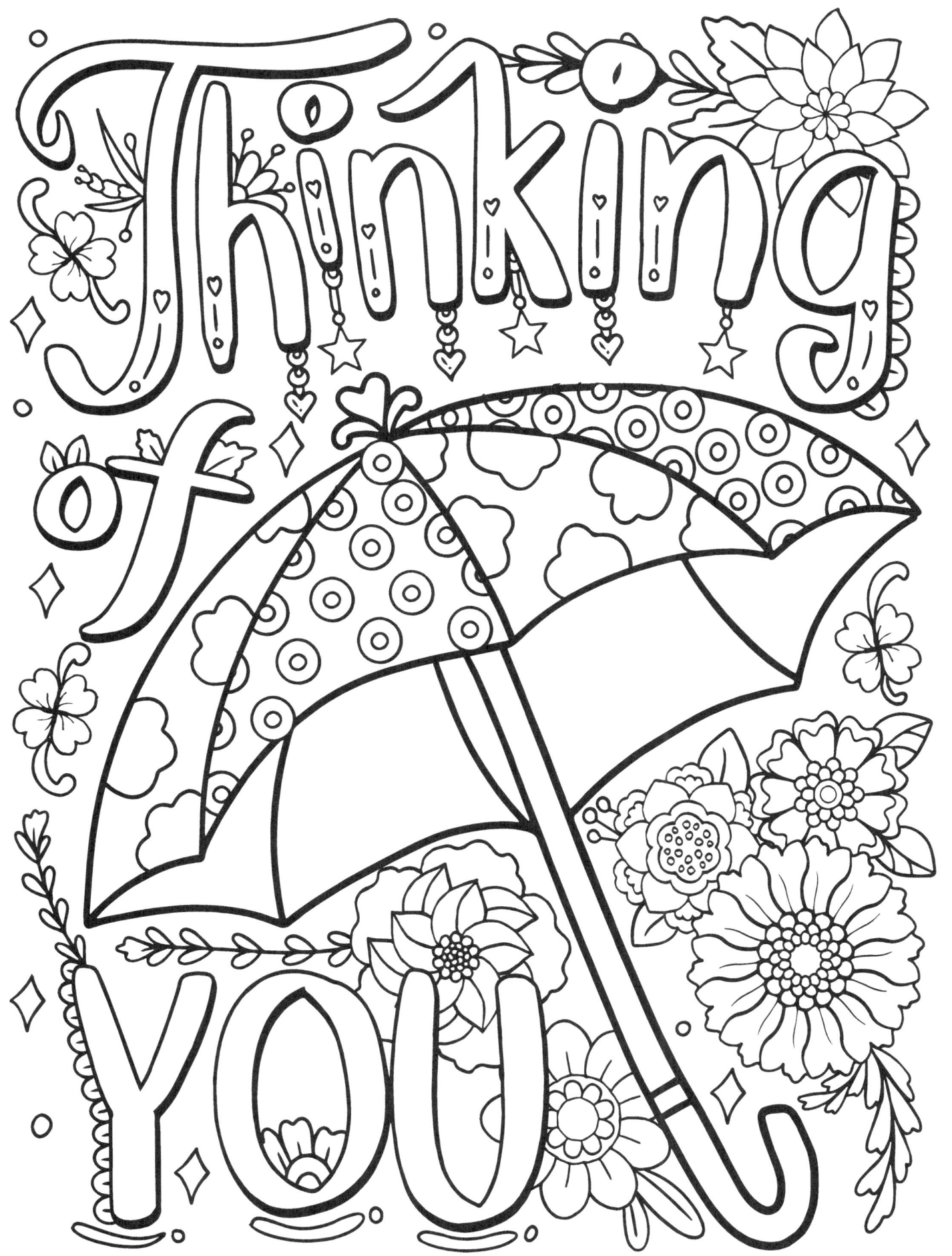

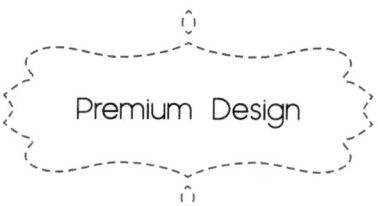

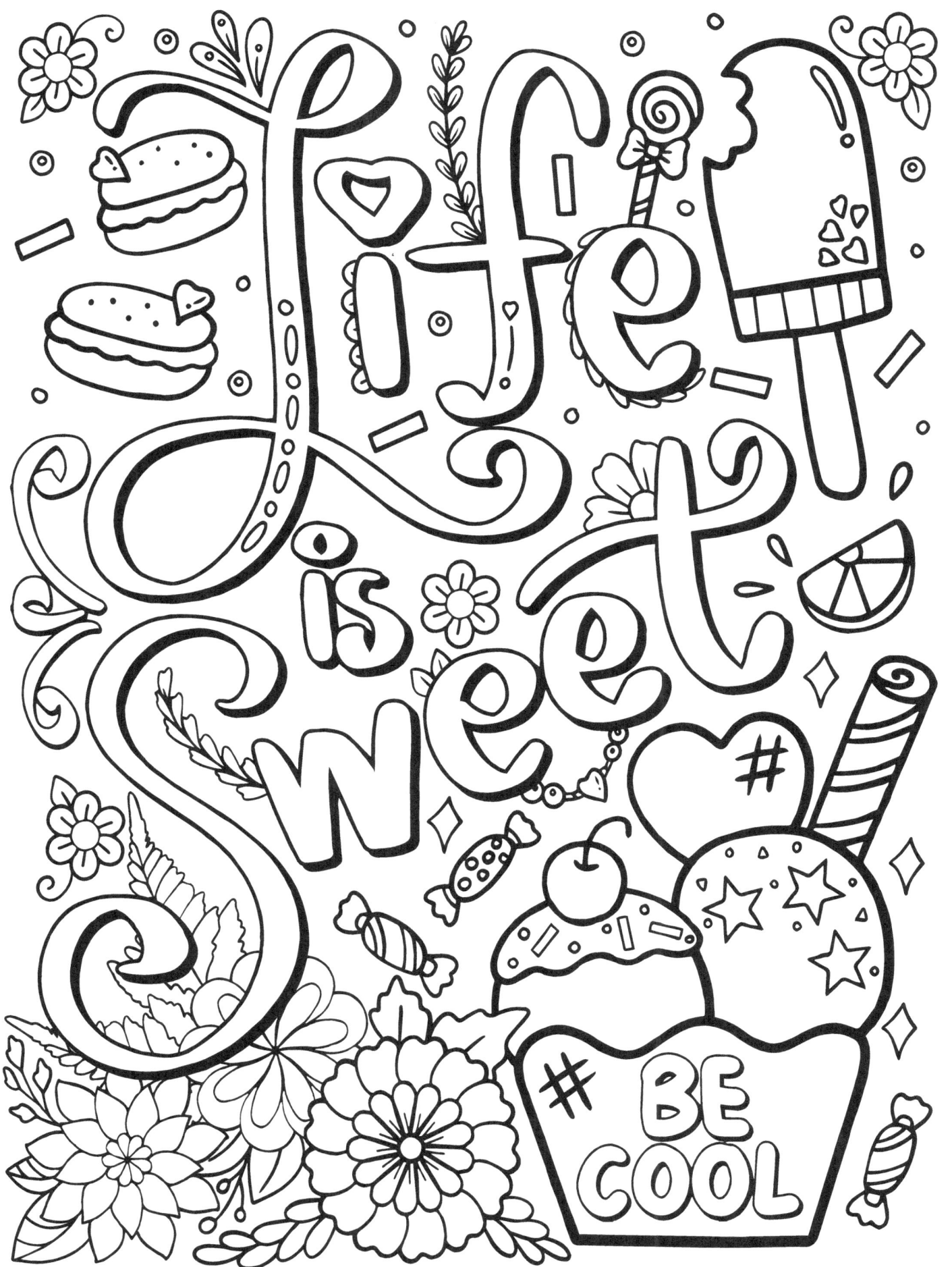

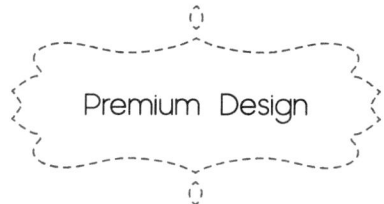

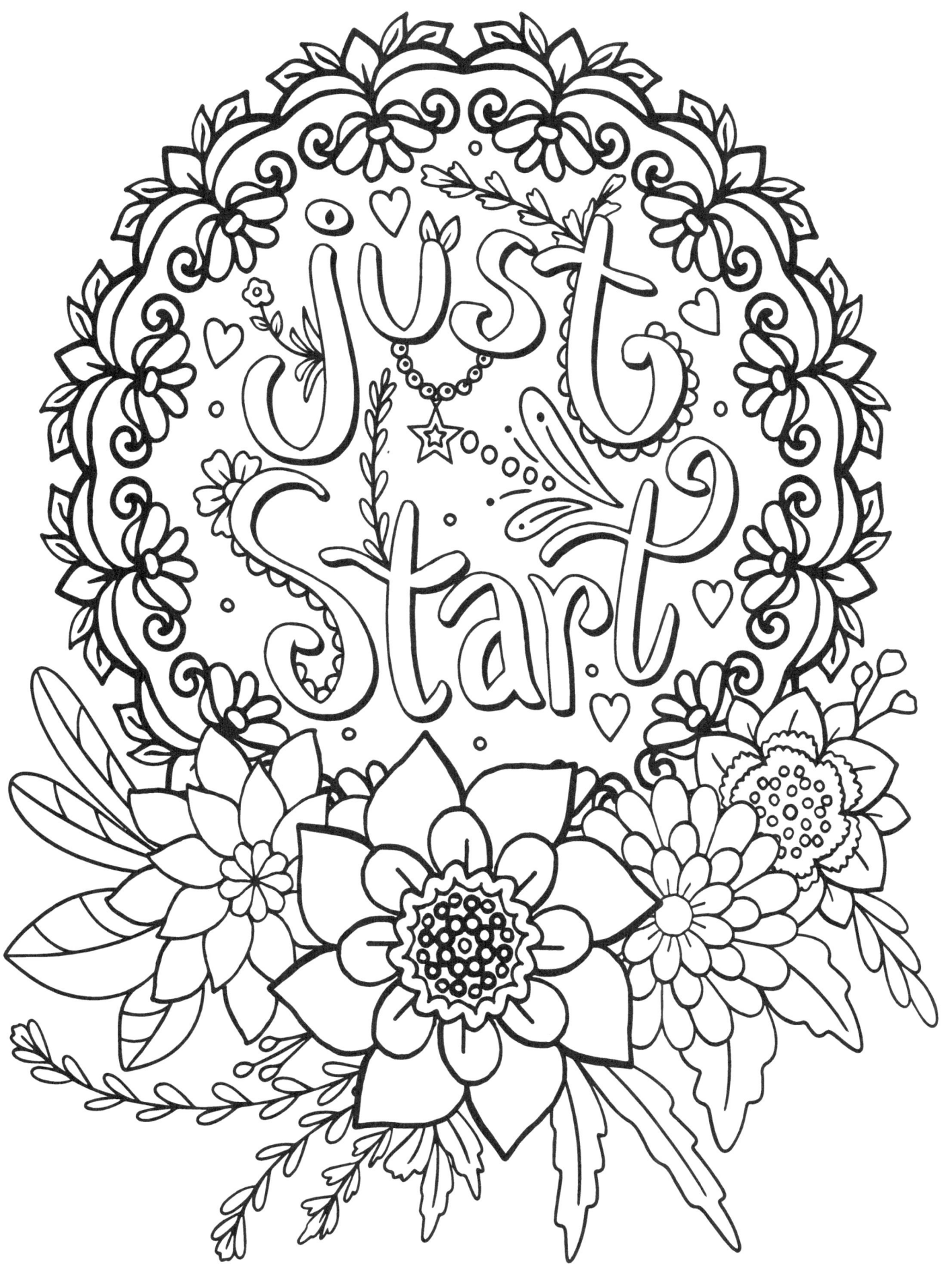

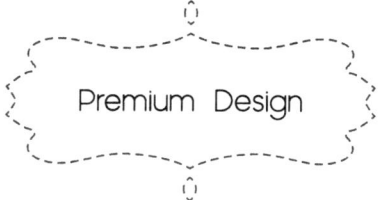

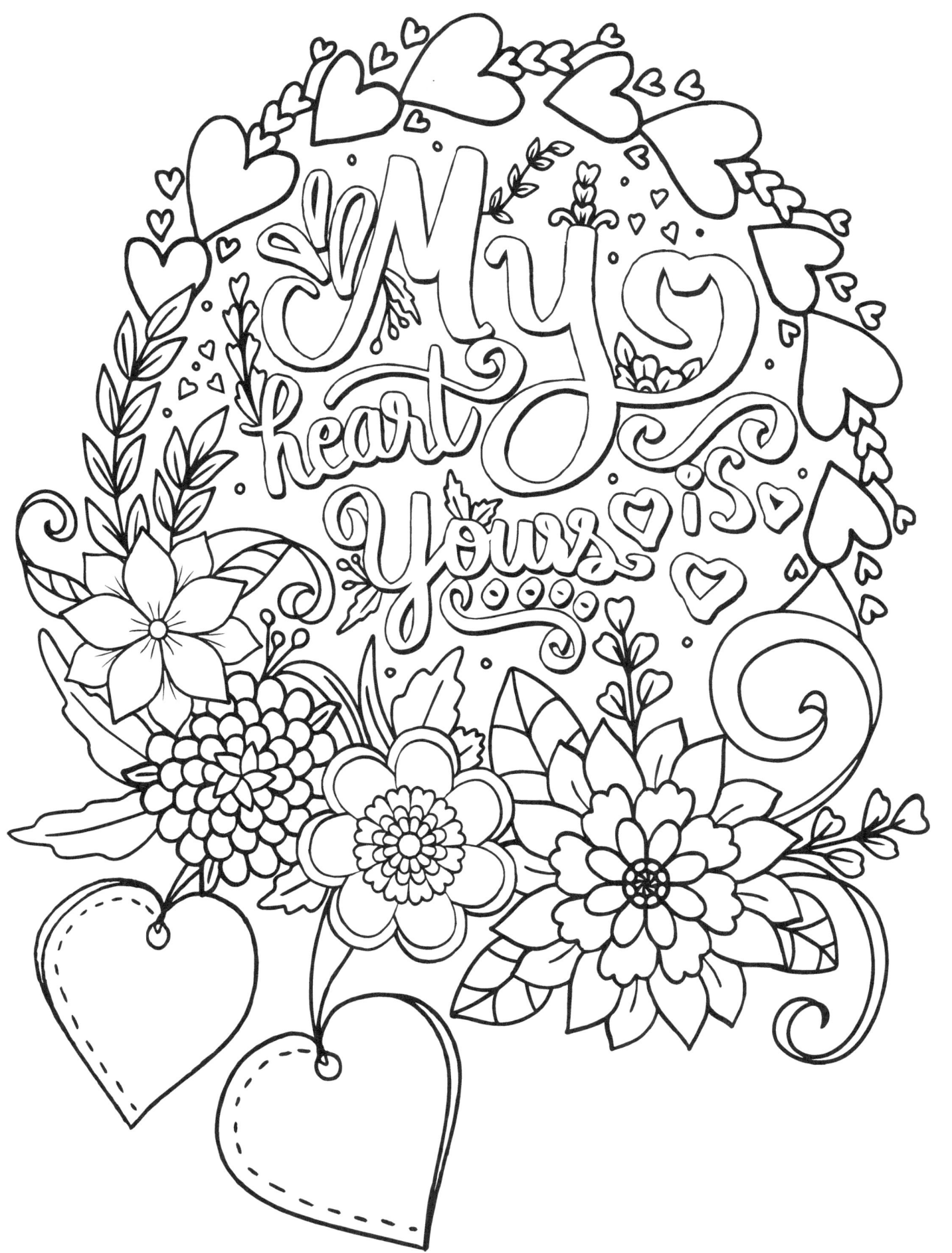

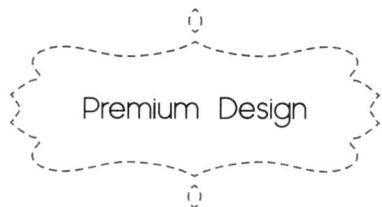

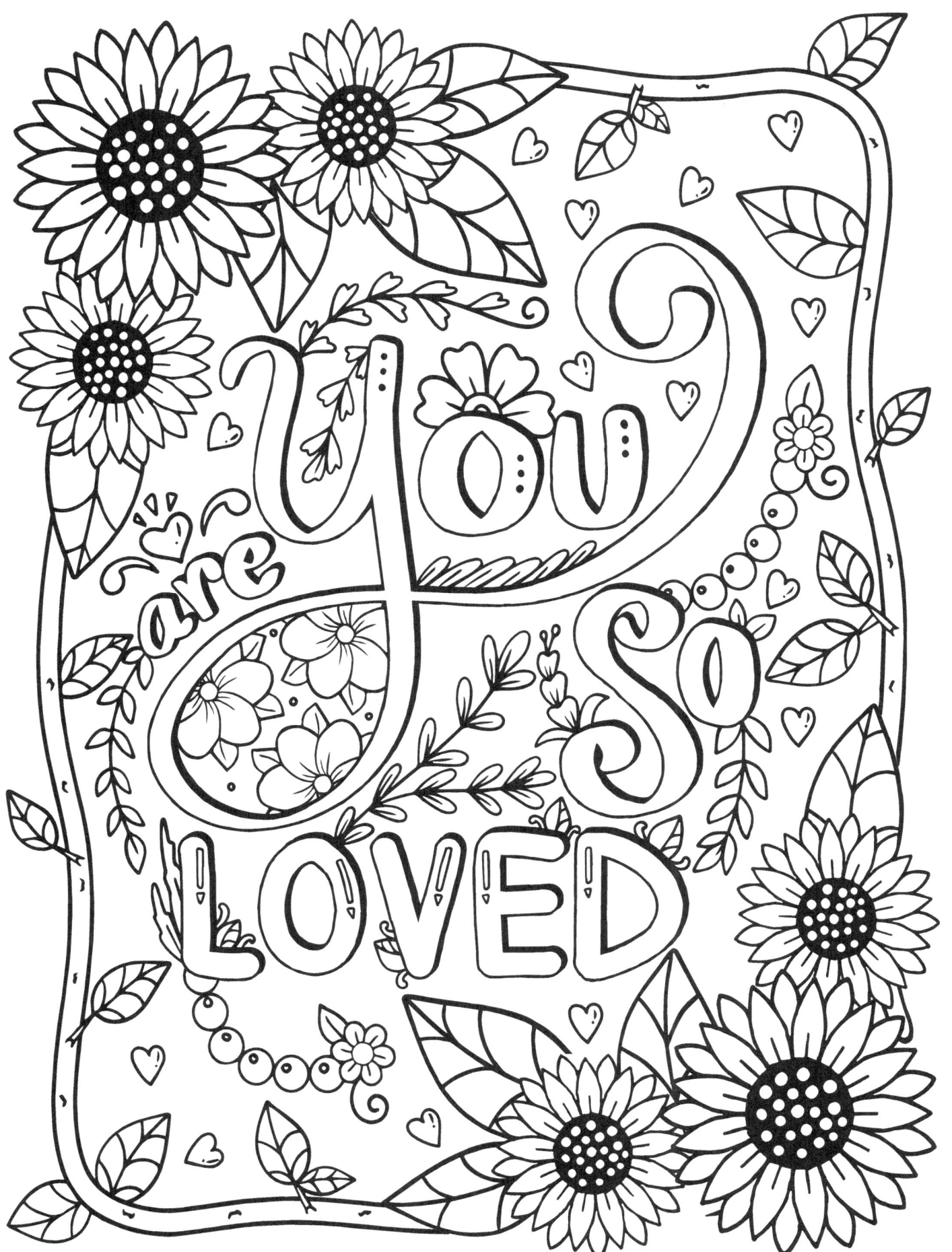

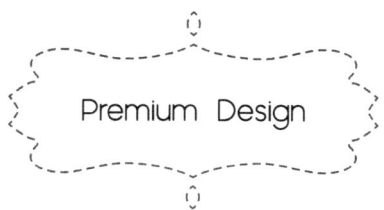

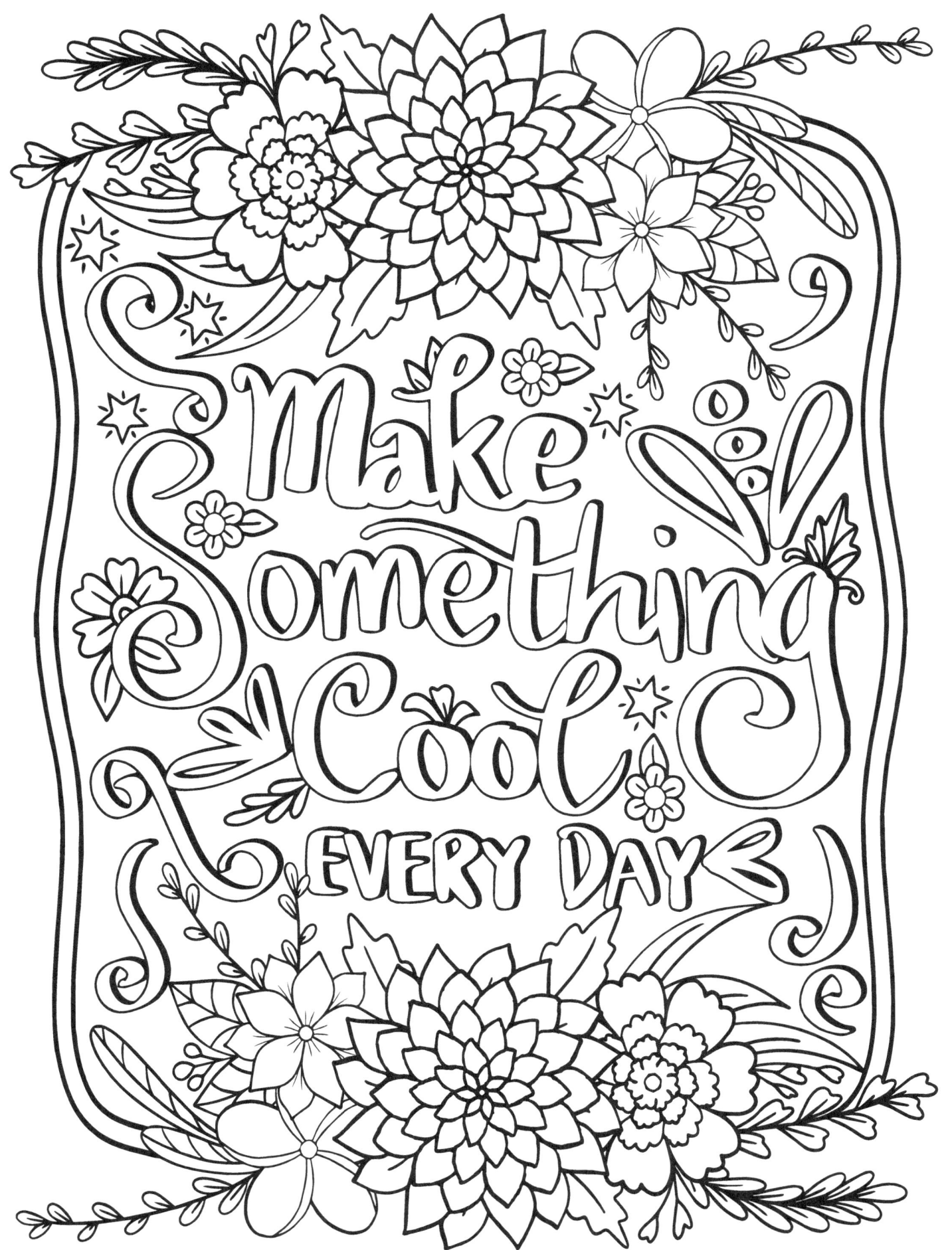

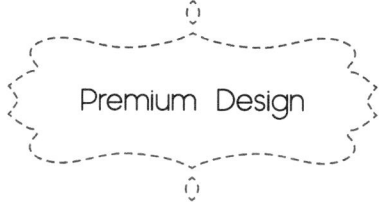
Premium Design

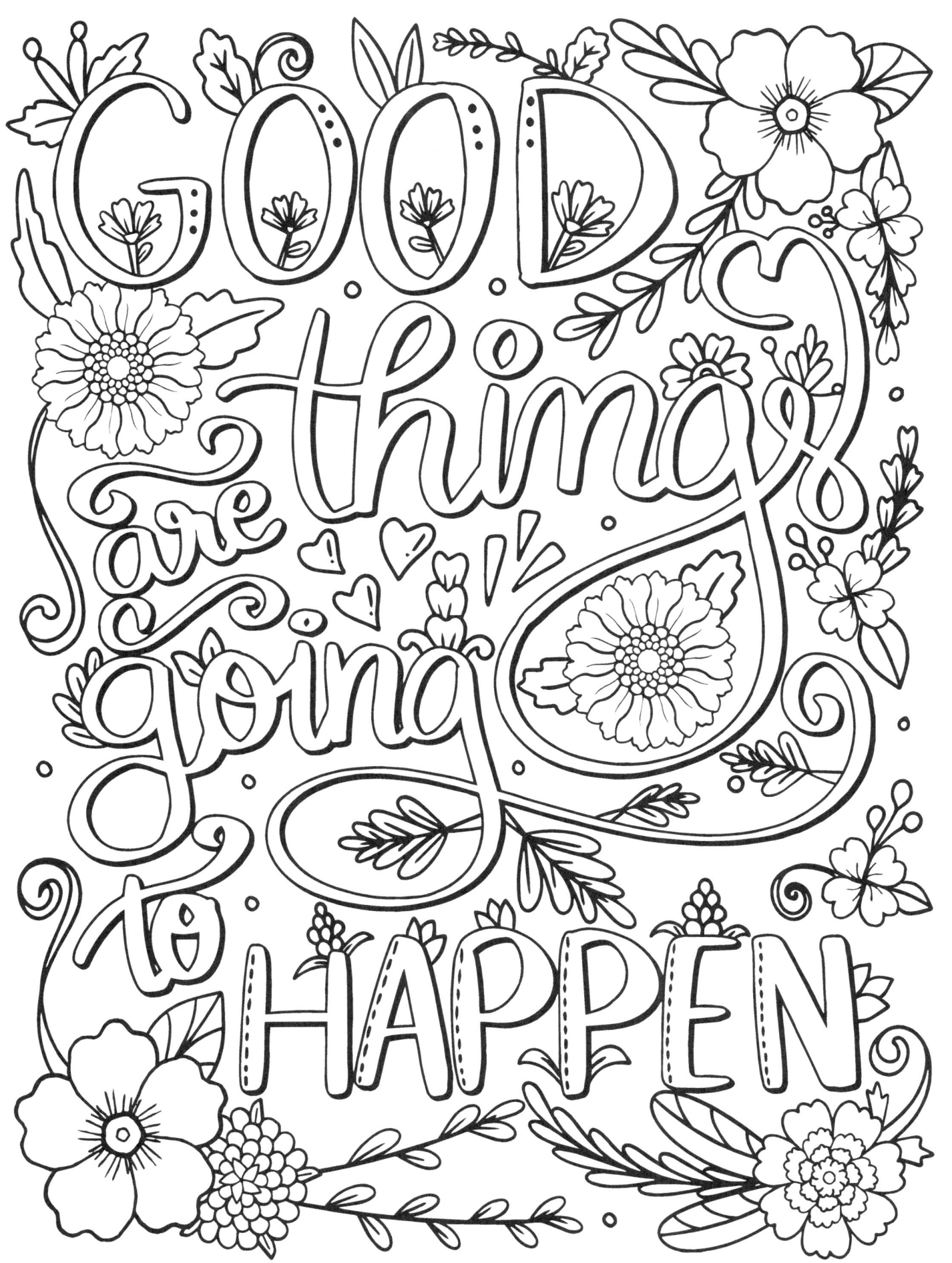

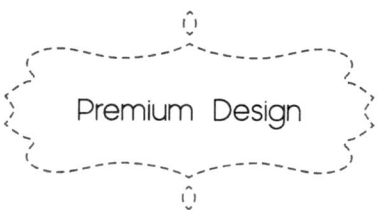

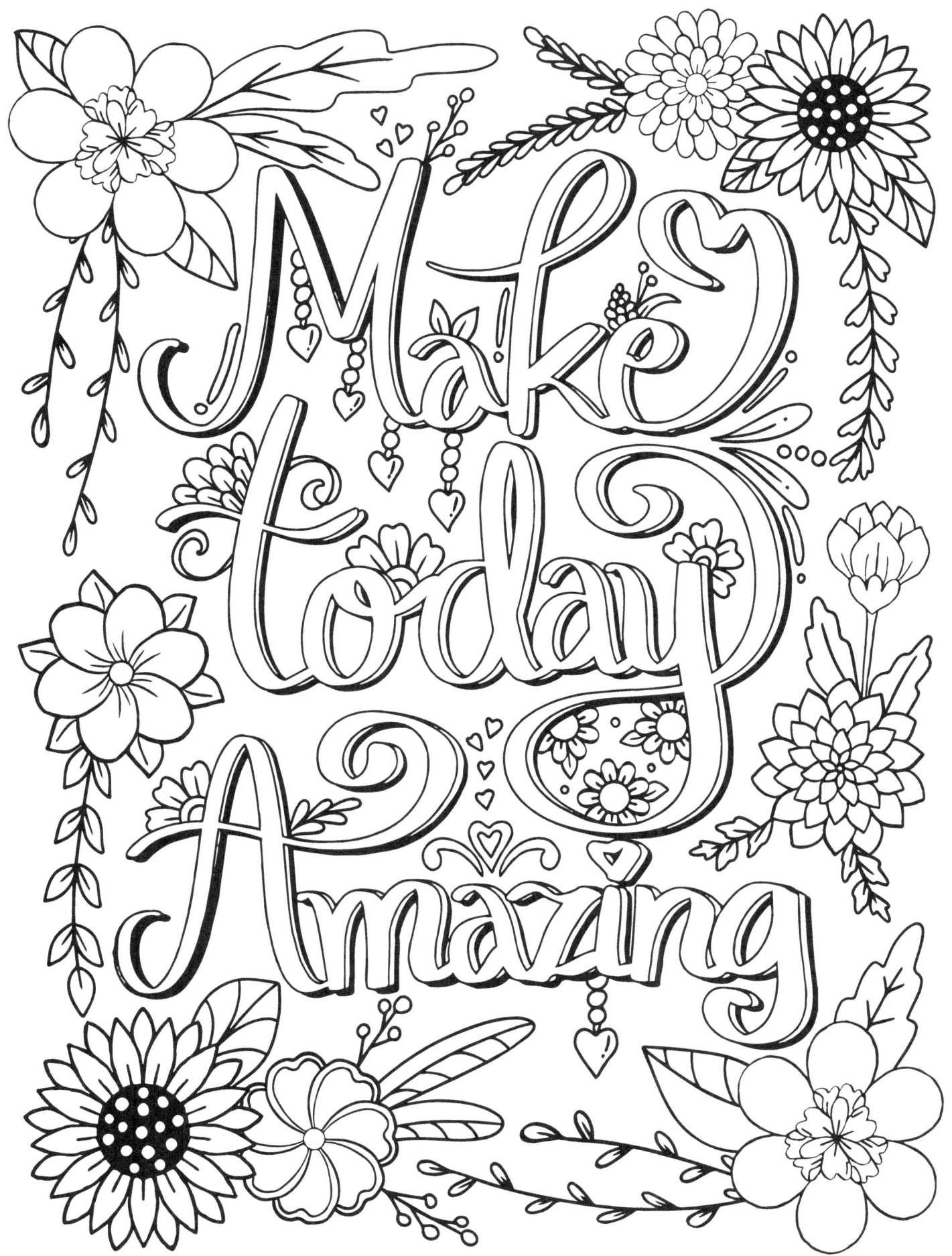

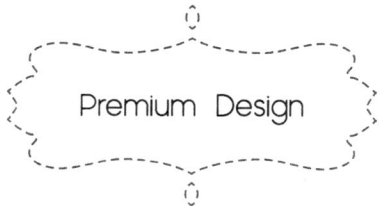

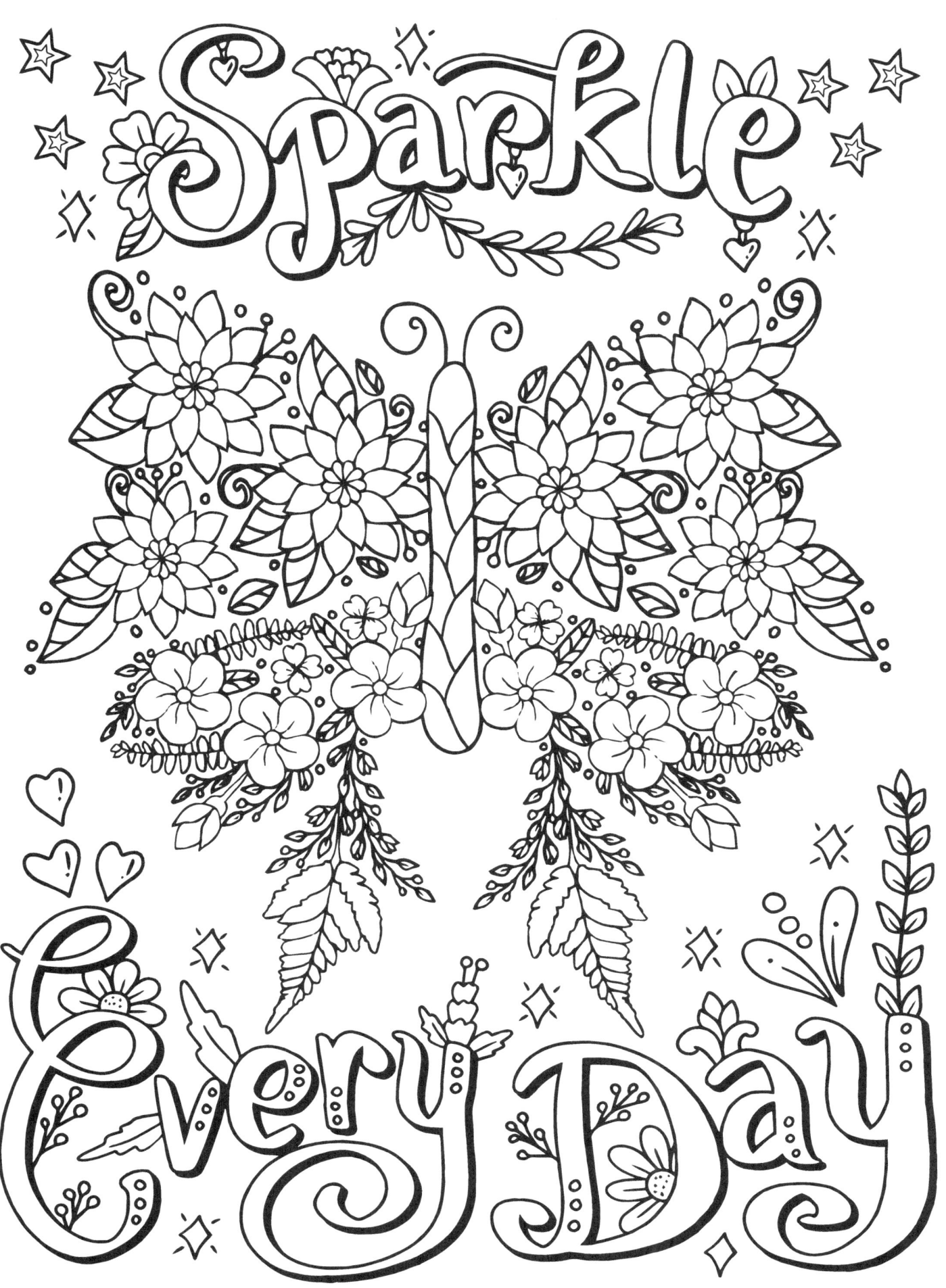

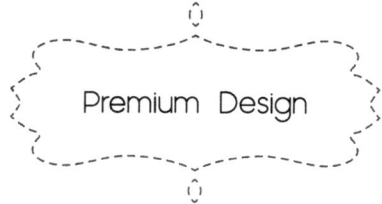

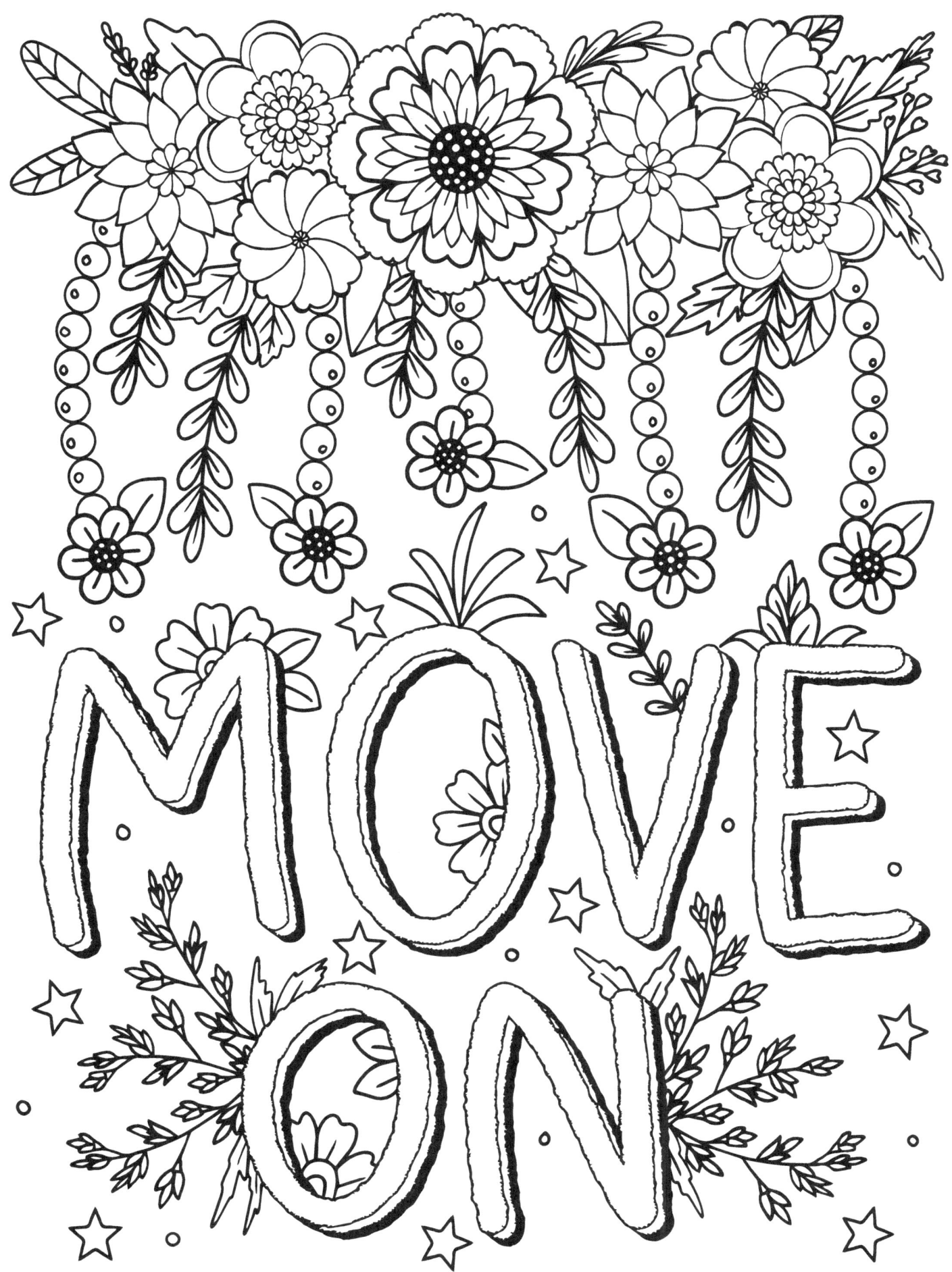

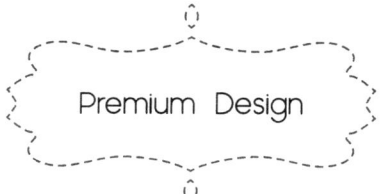

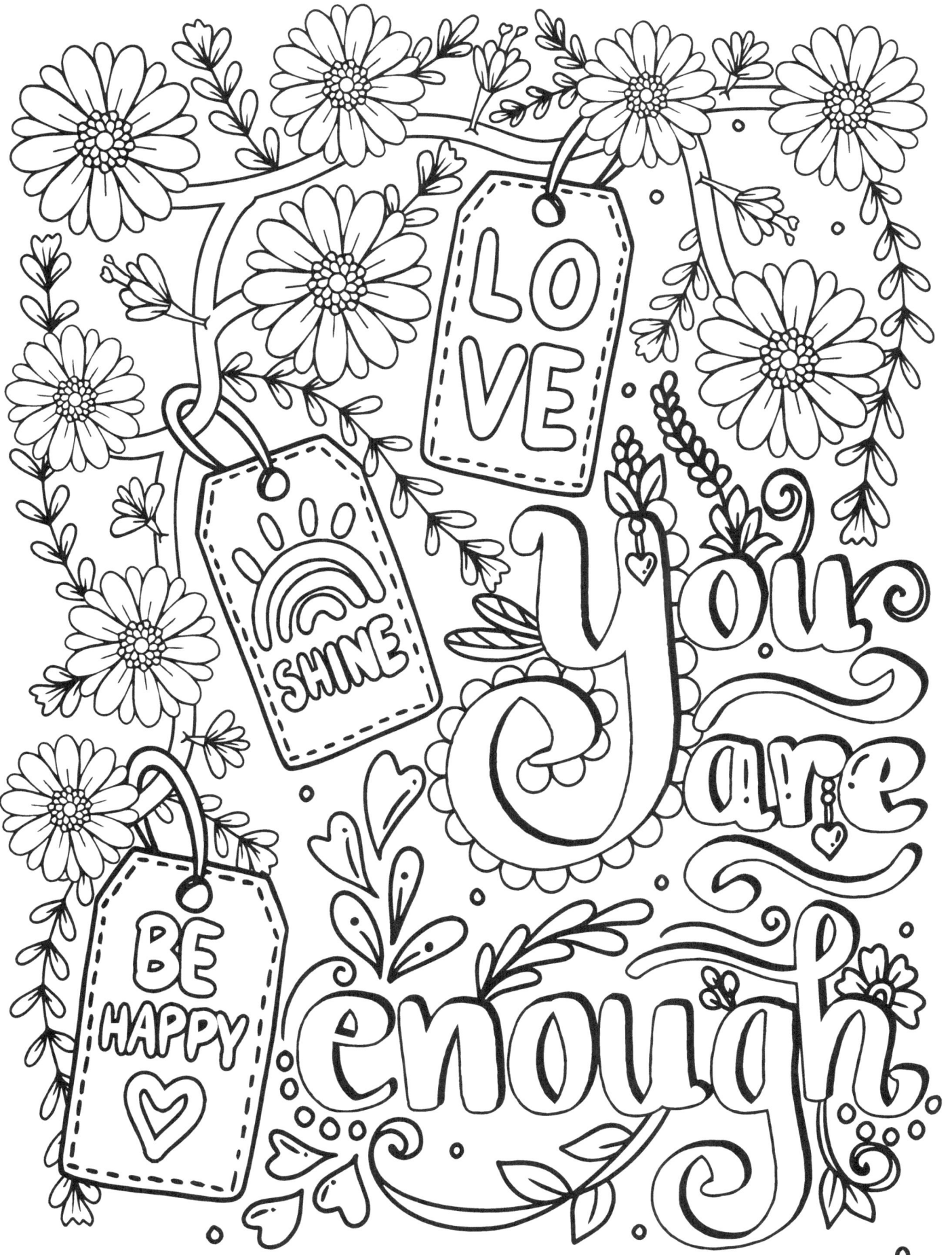

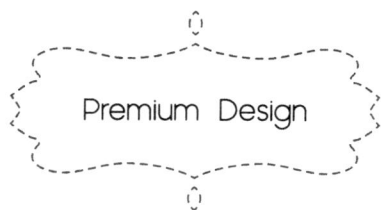

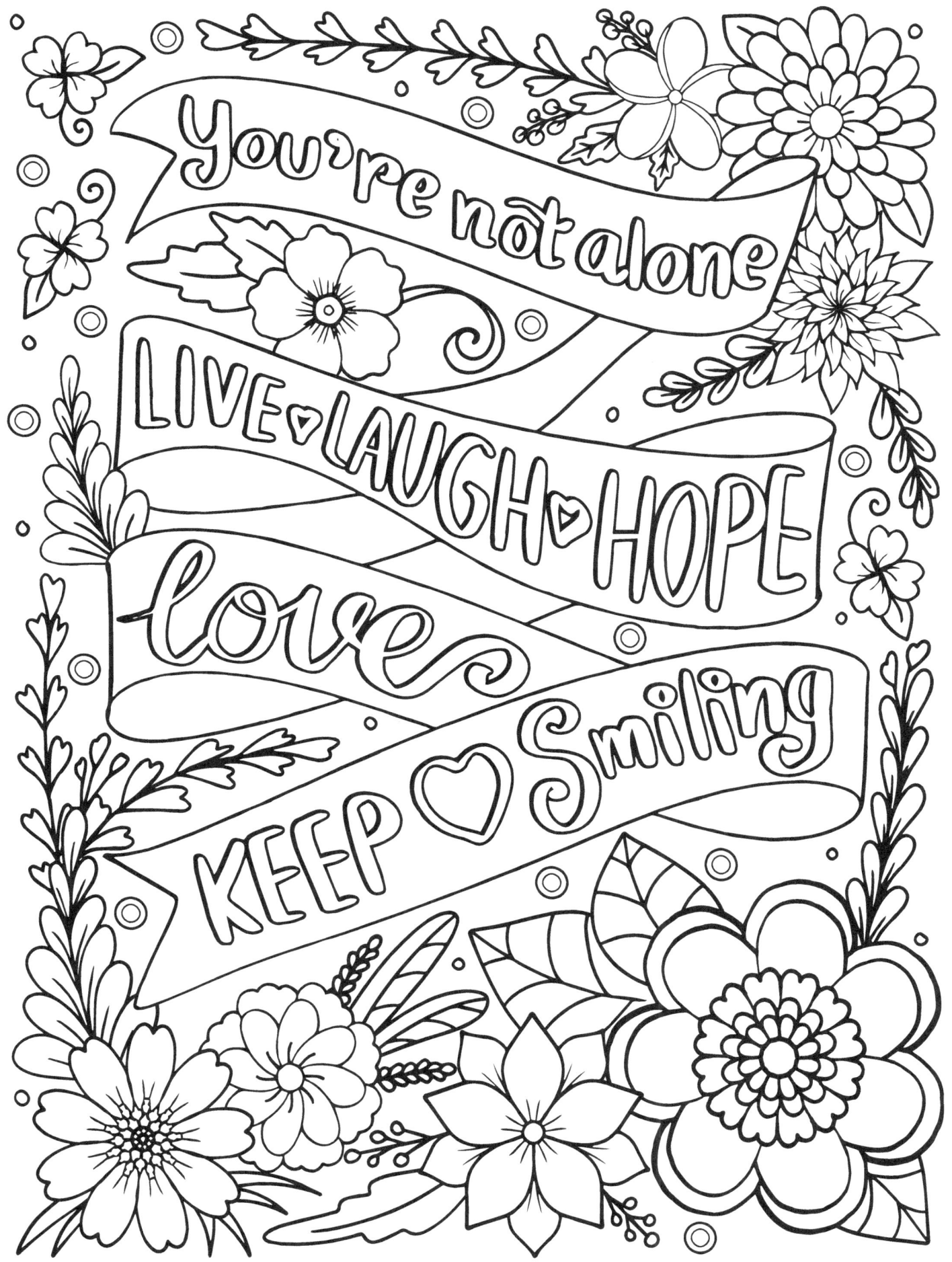

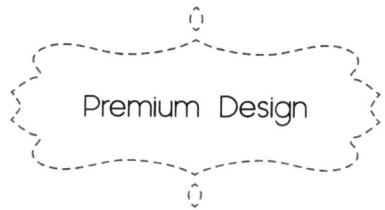

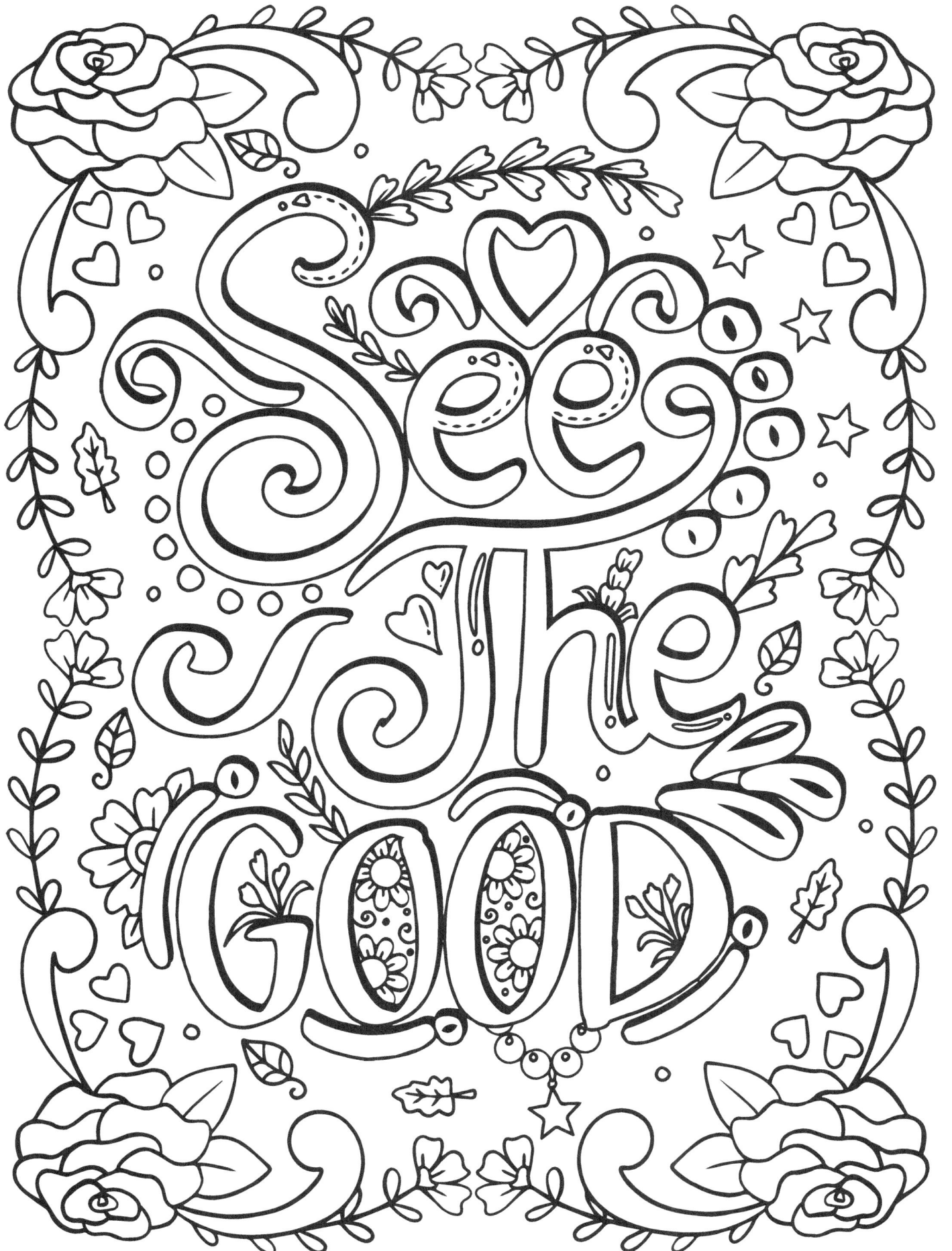

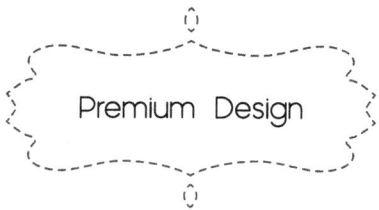

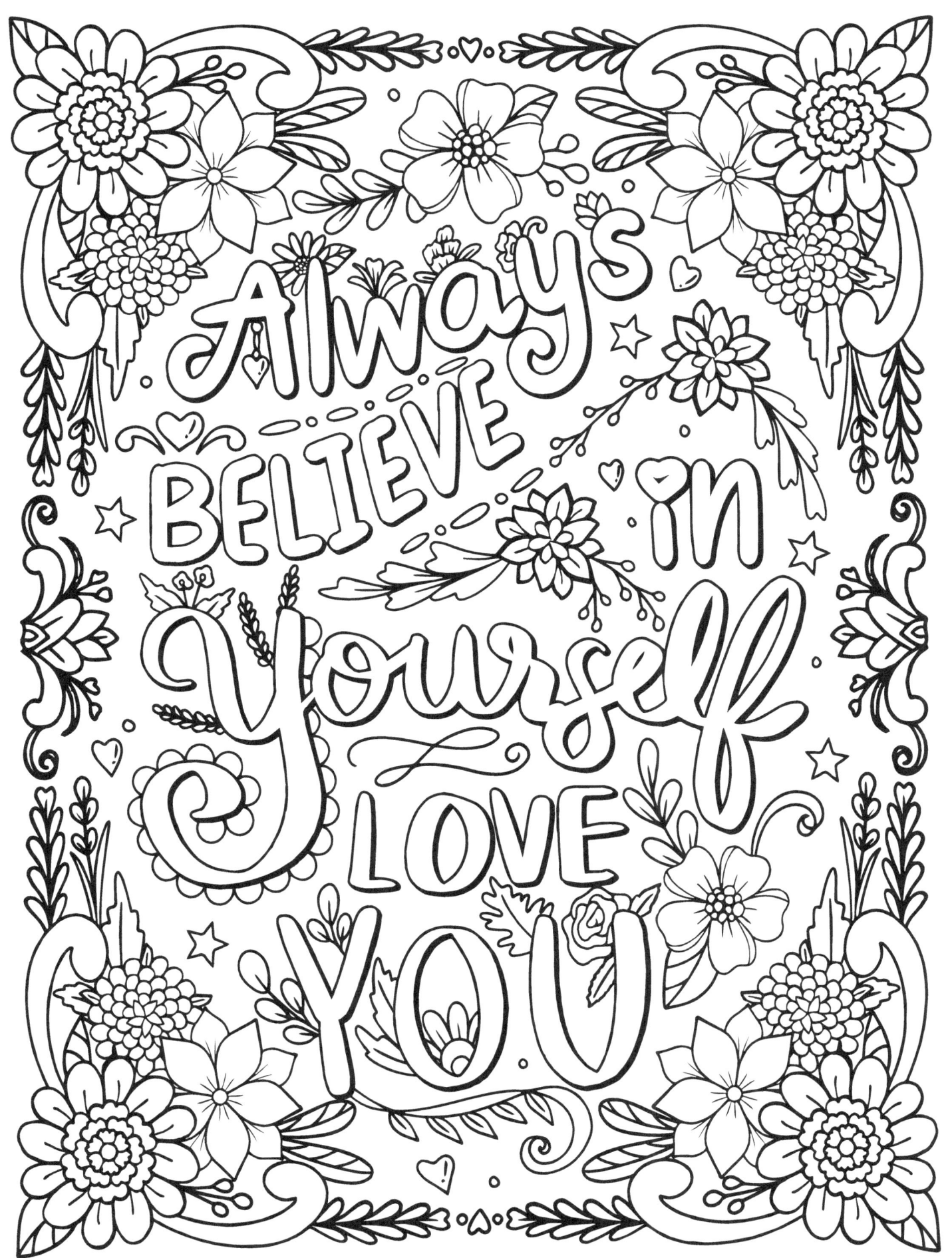

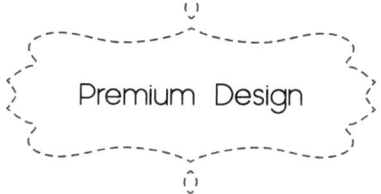

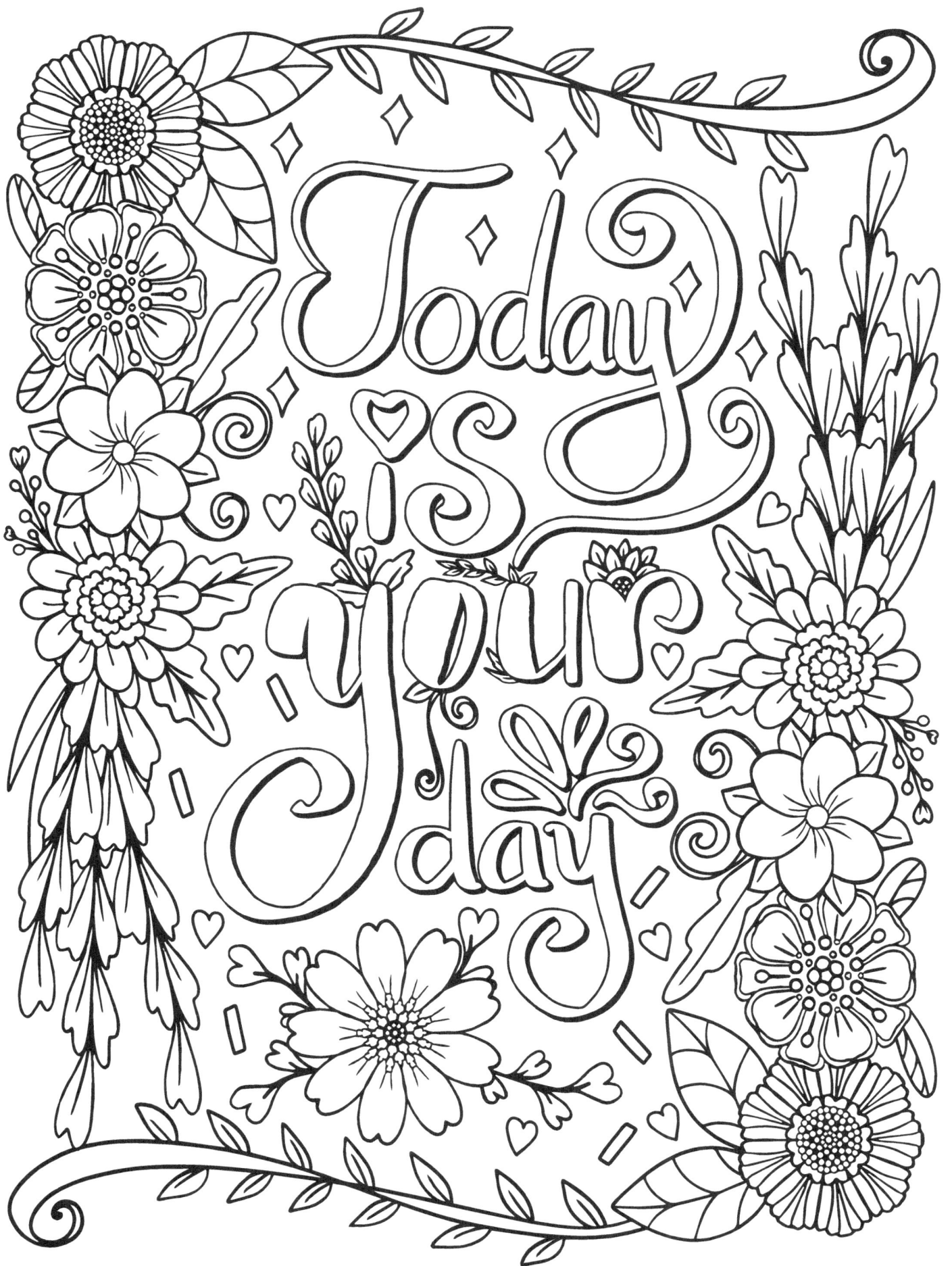

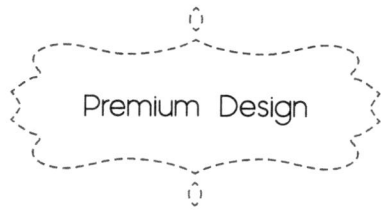

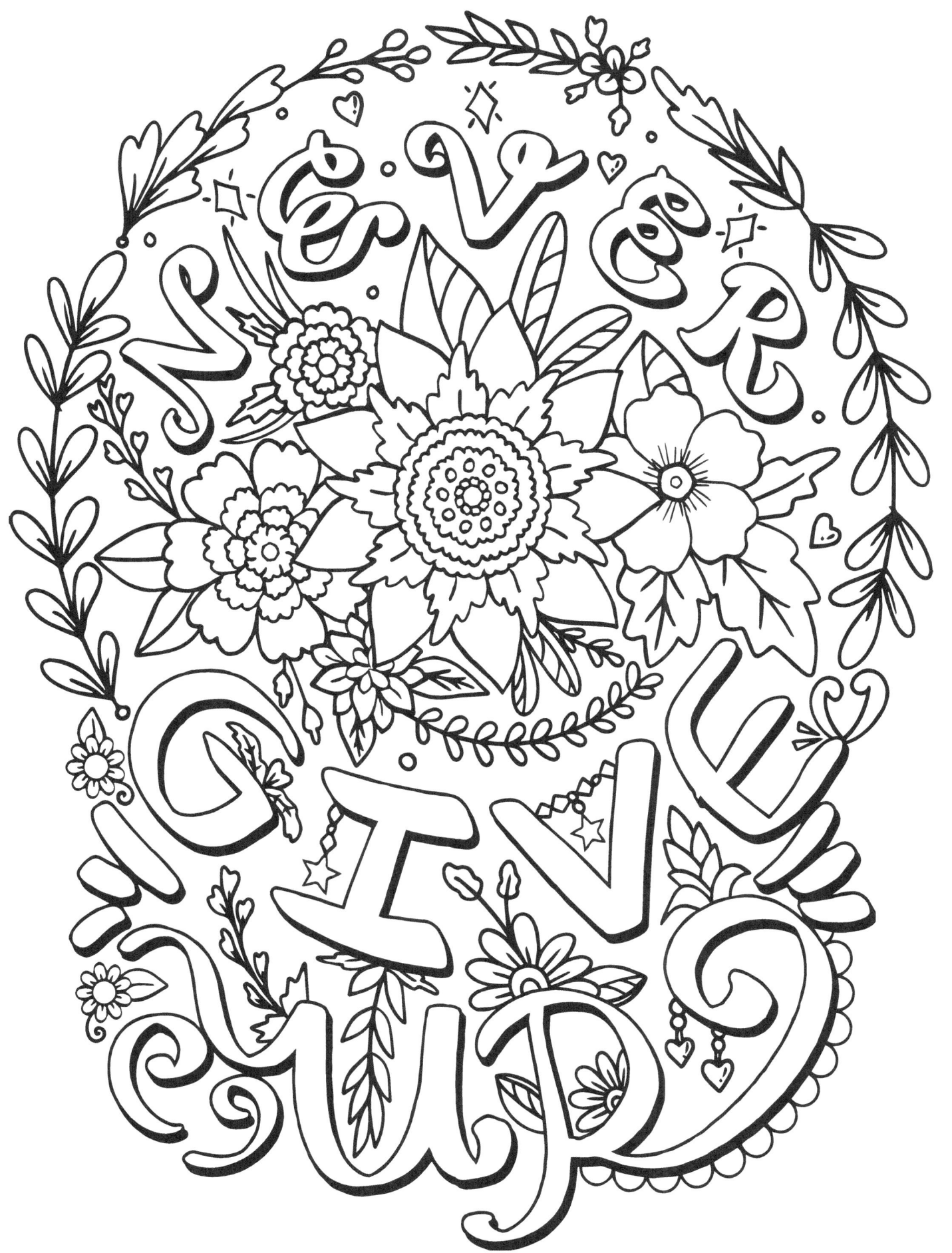

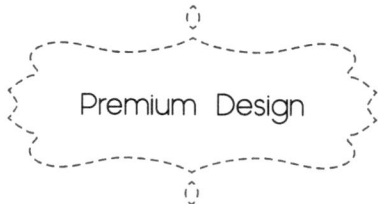

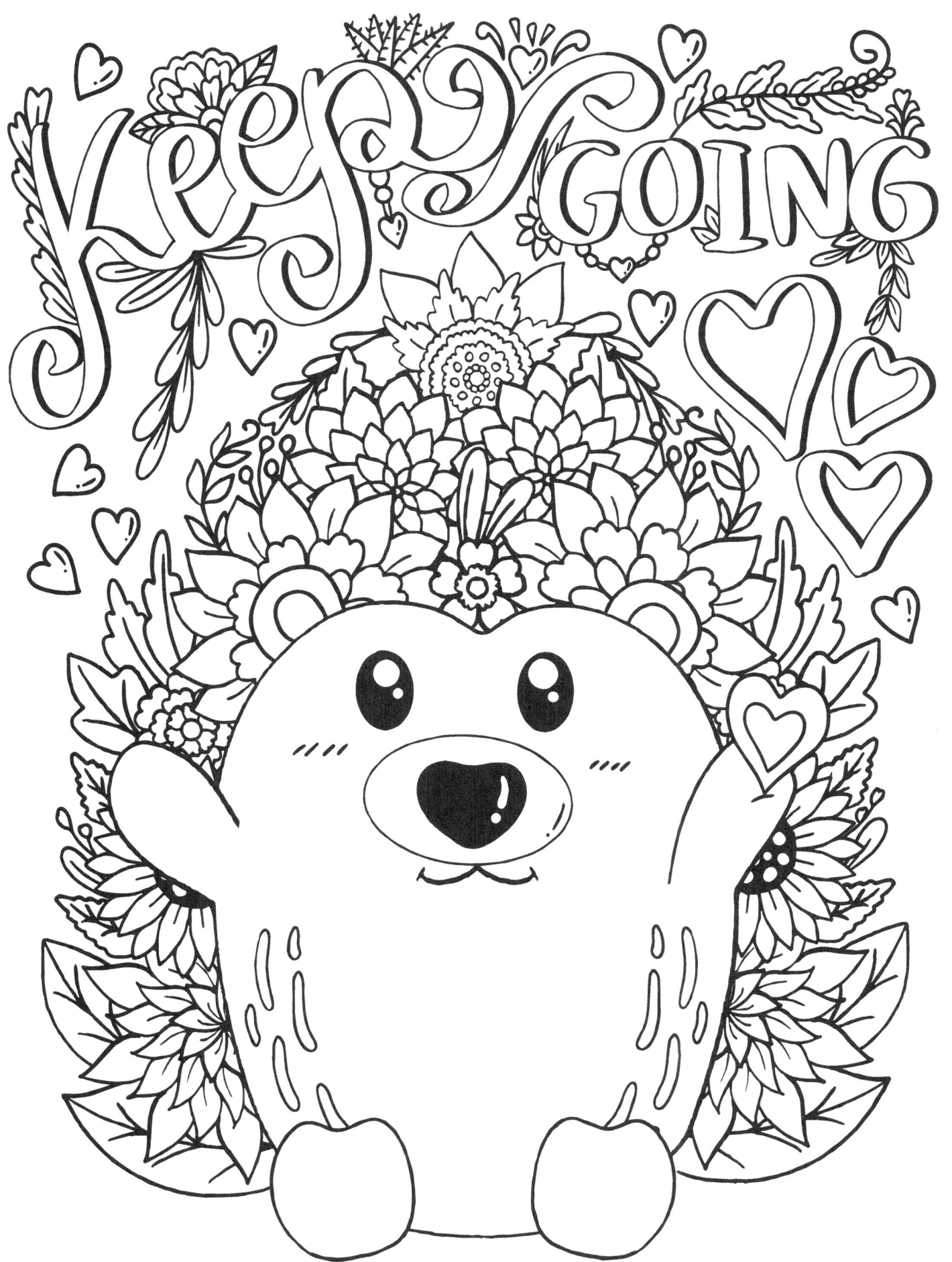

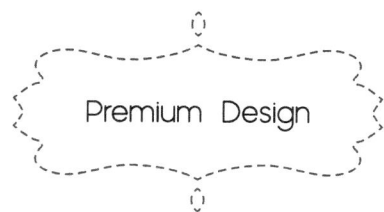

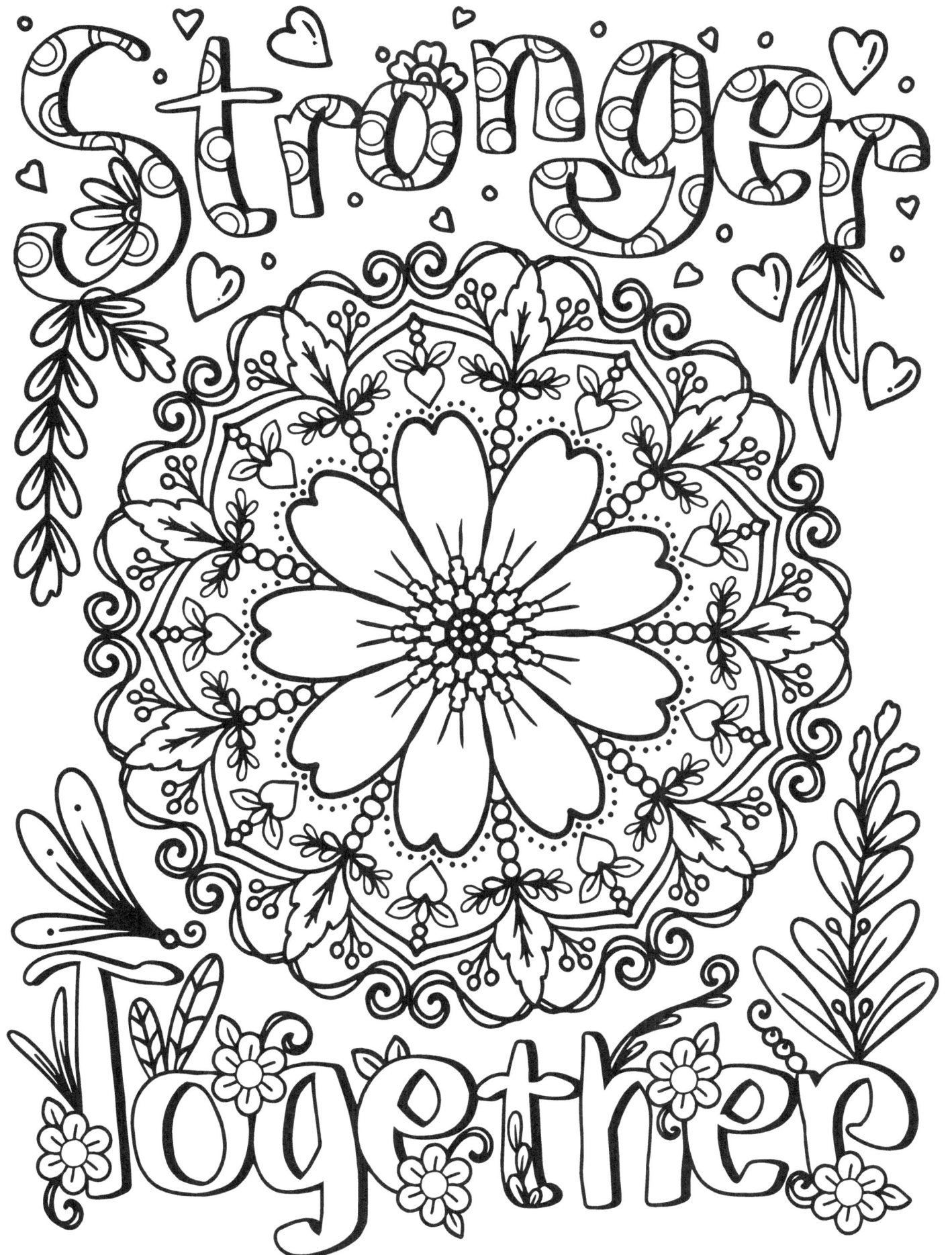

Premium Design

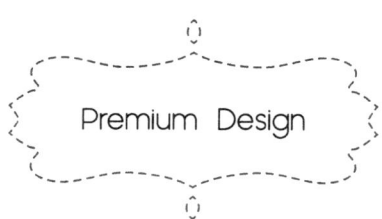

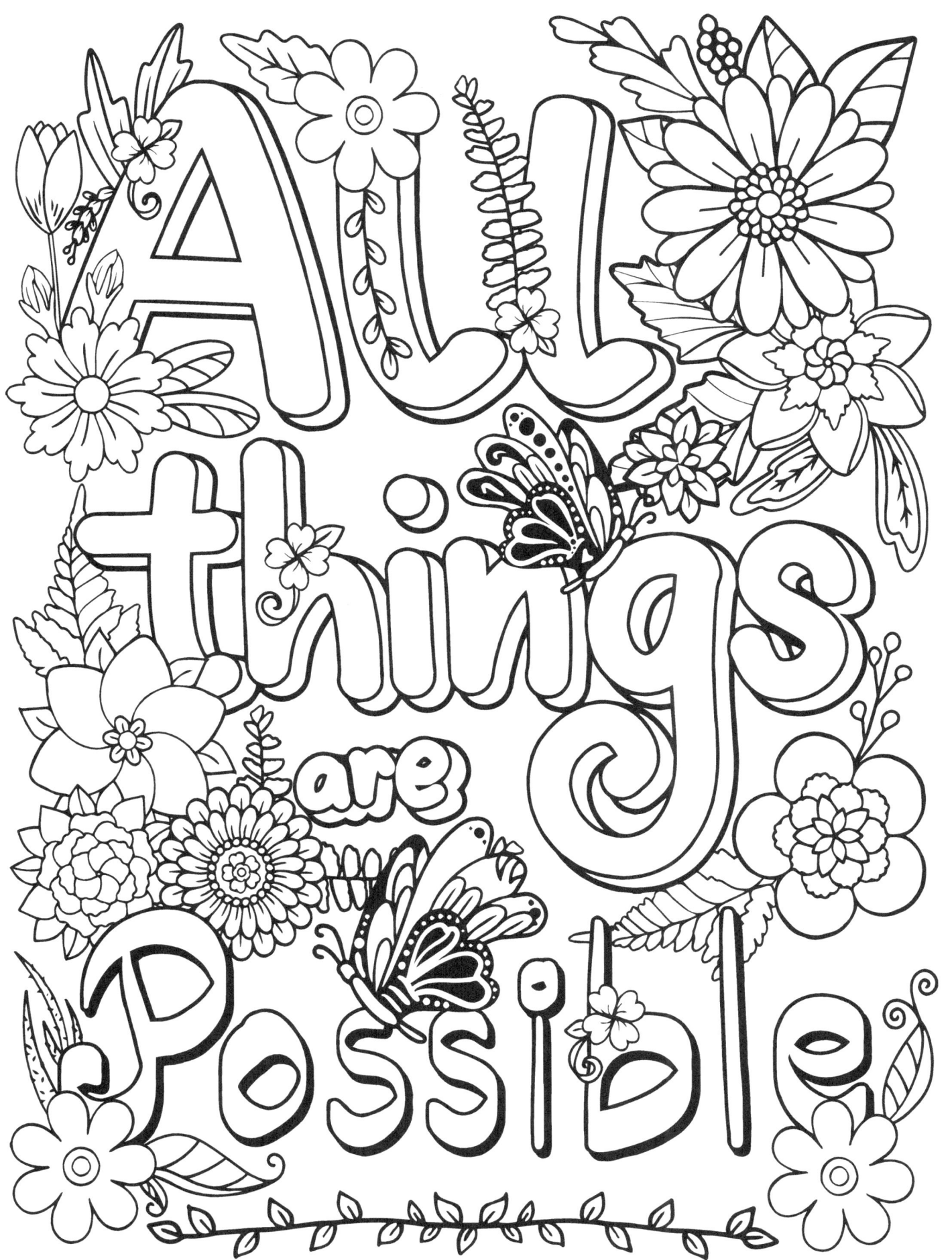

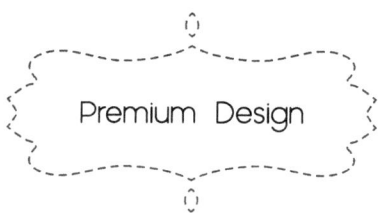

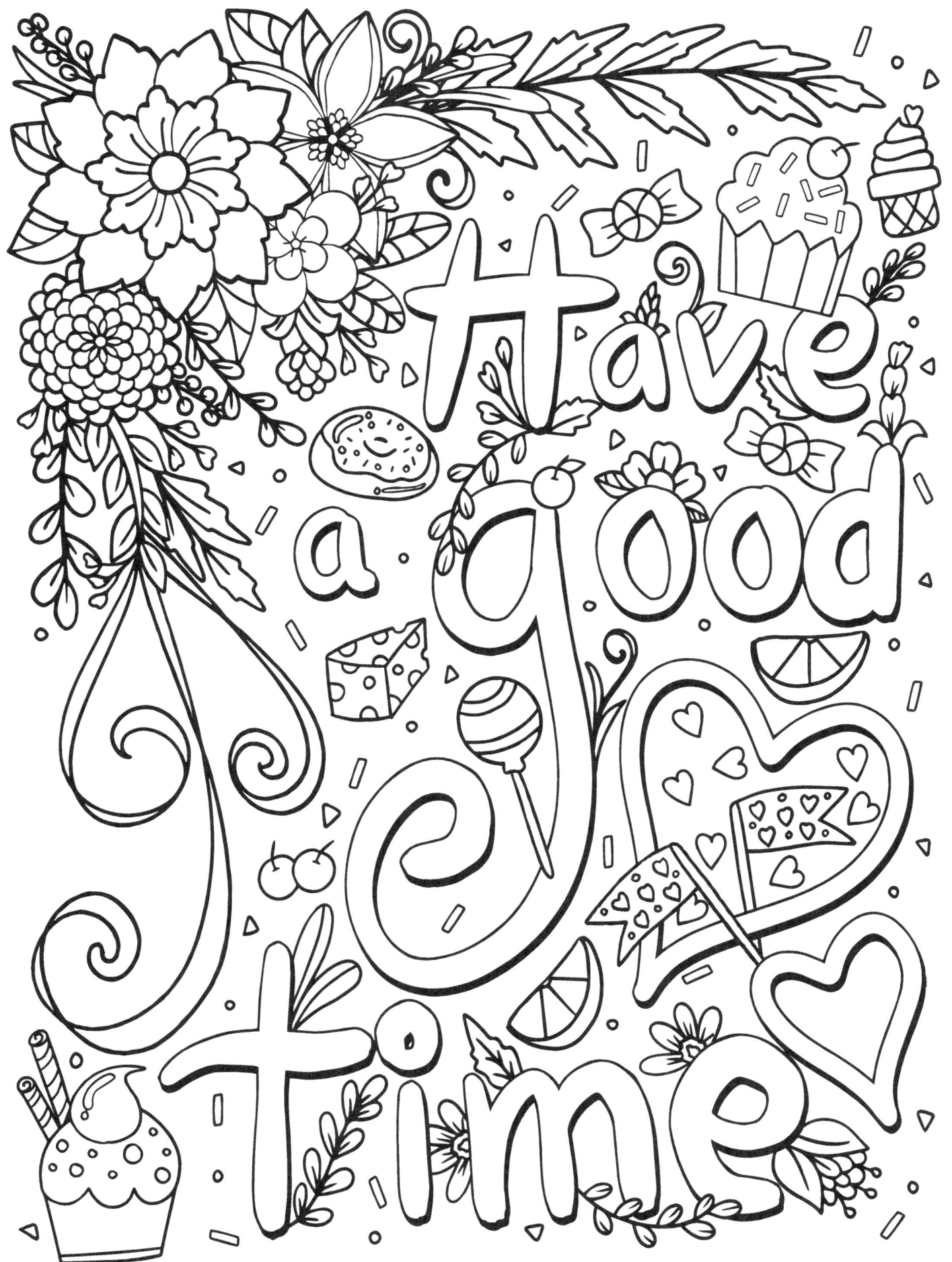

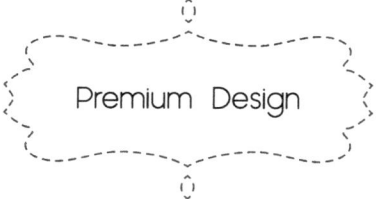

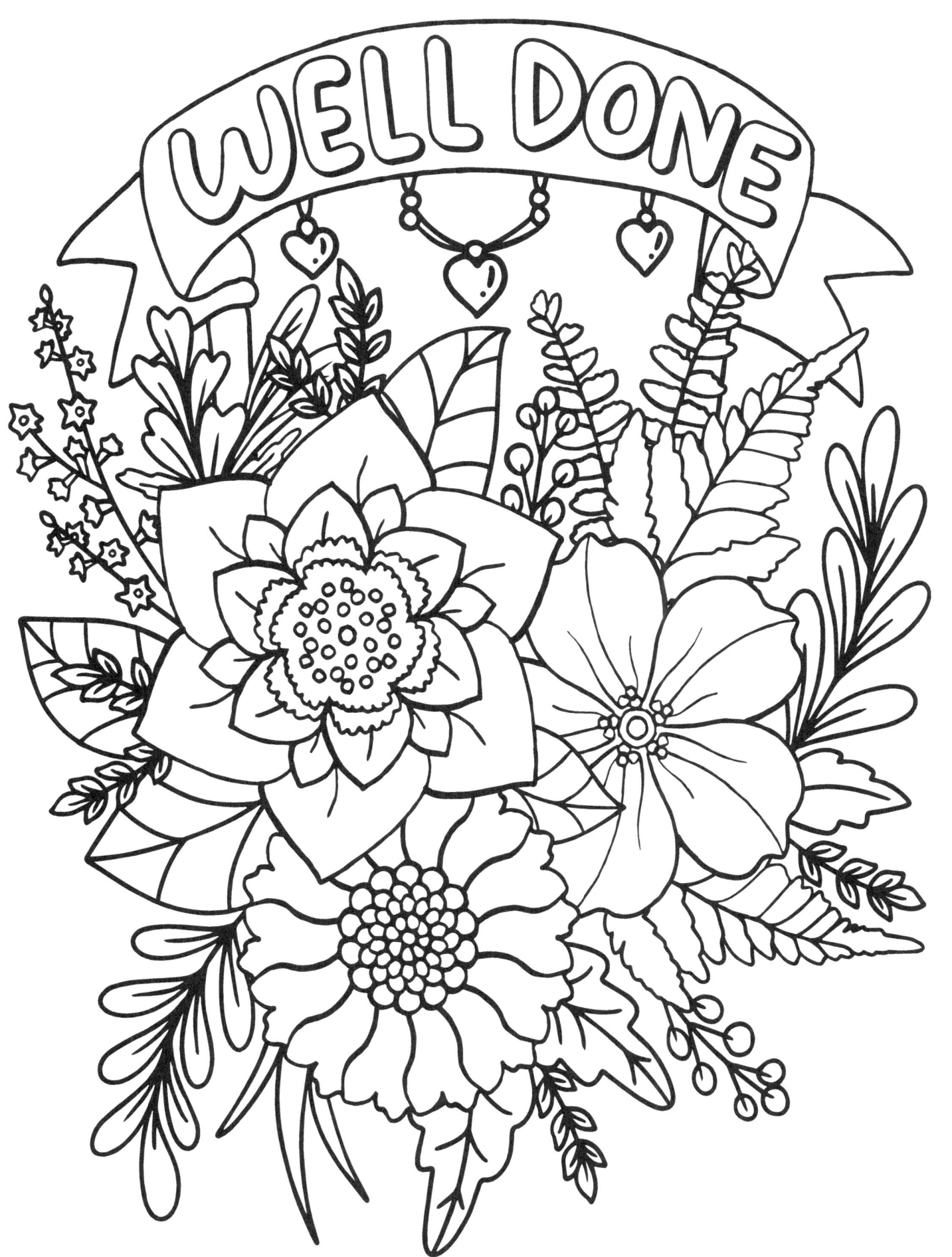

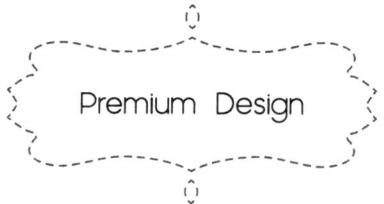

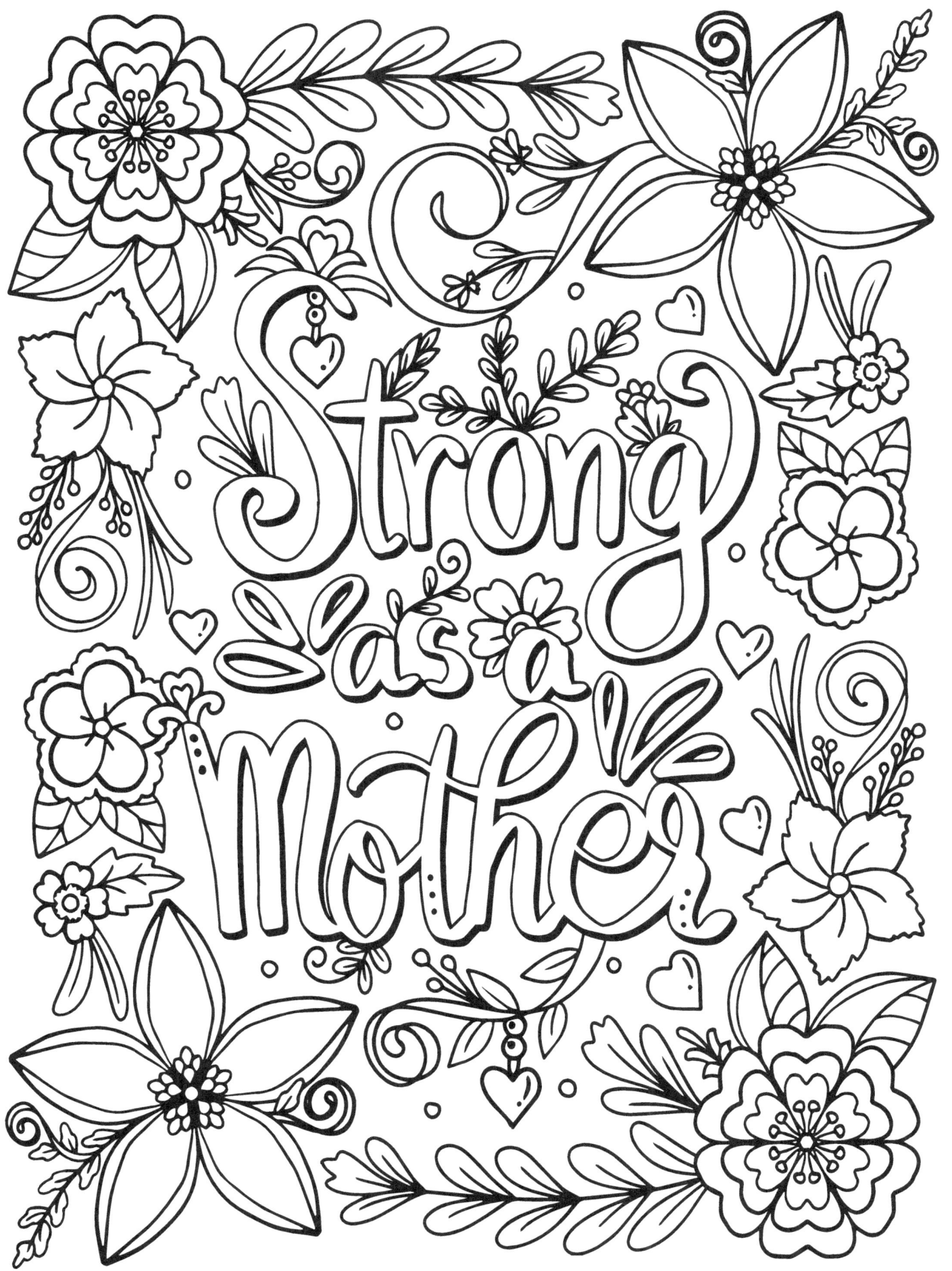

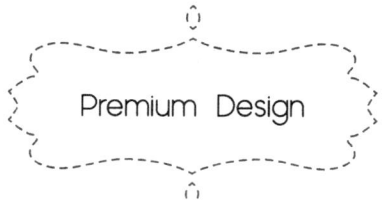
Premium Design

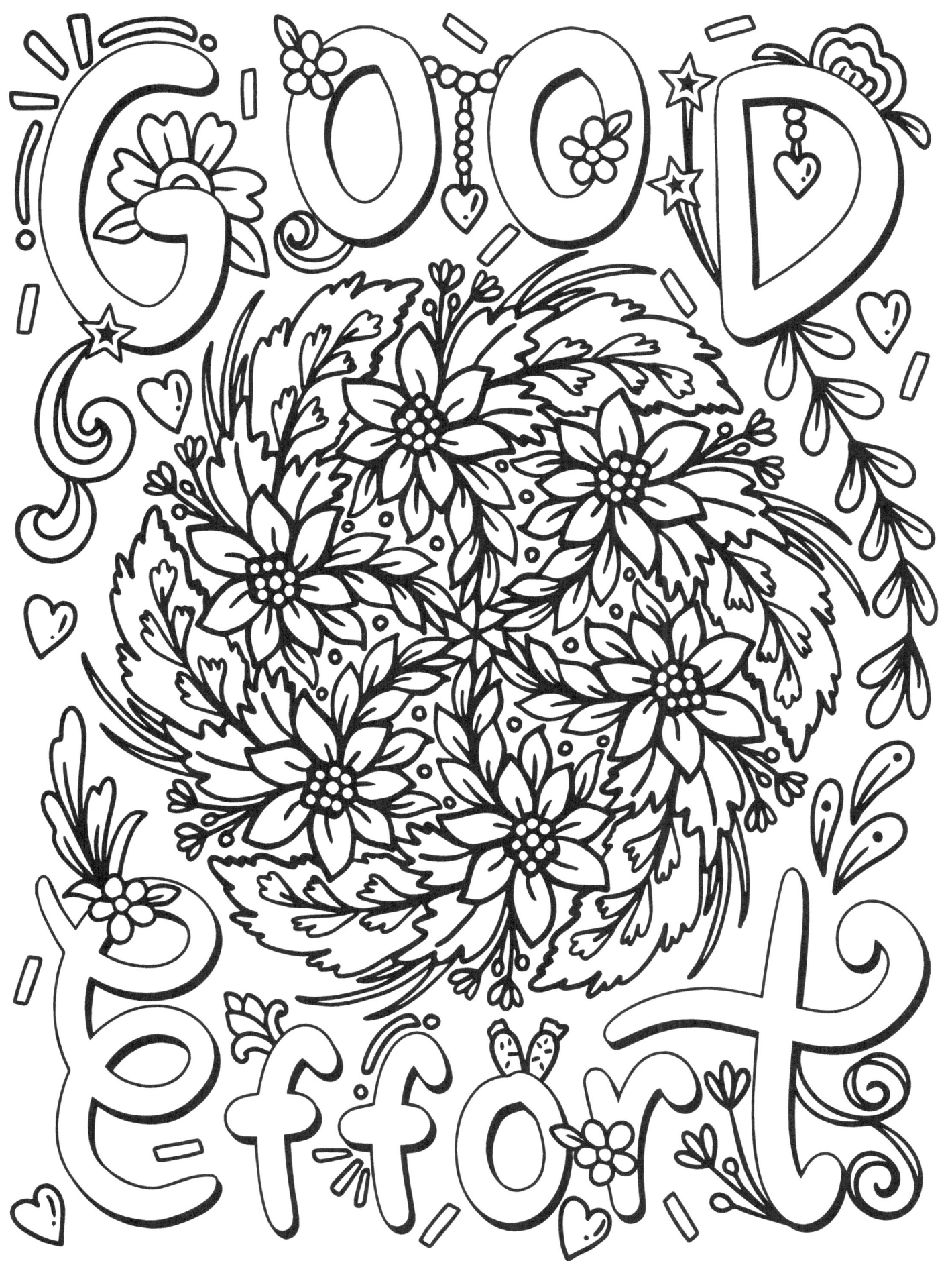

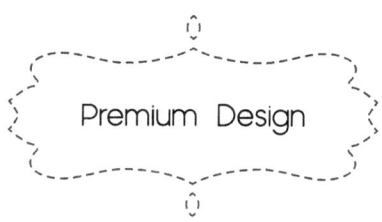

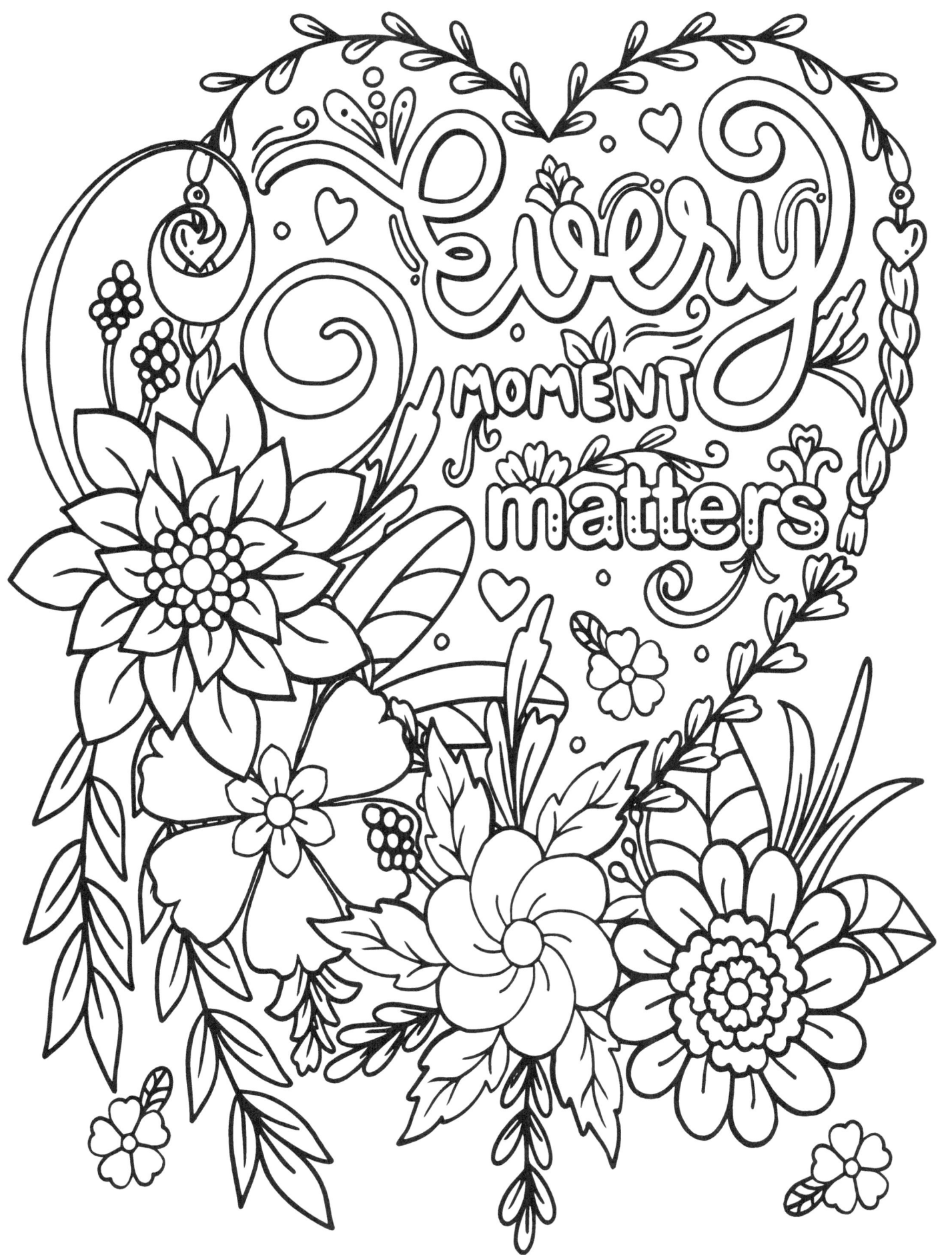

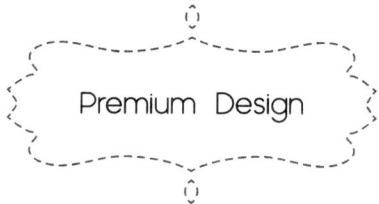

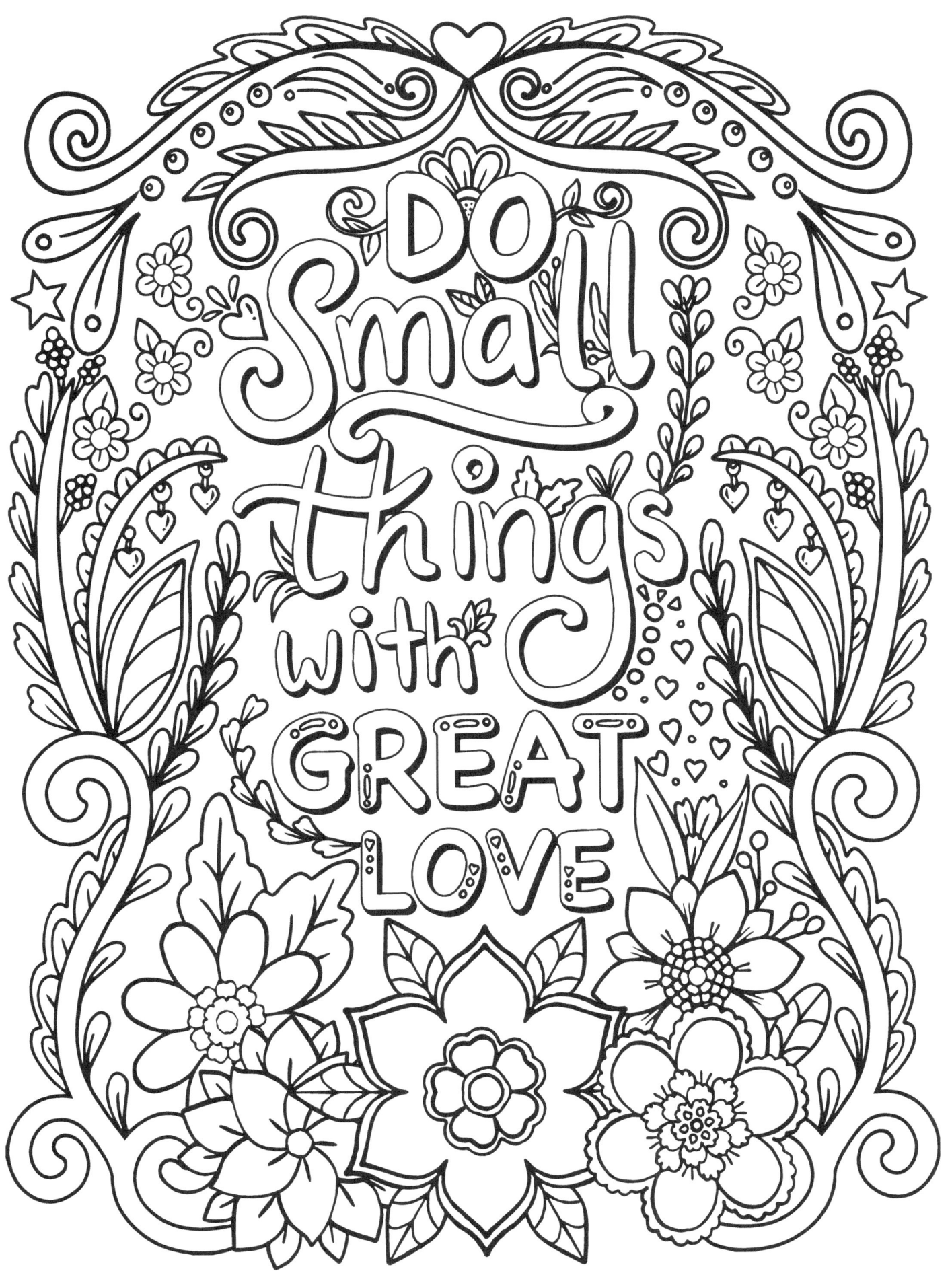

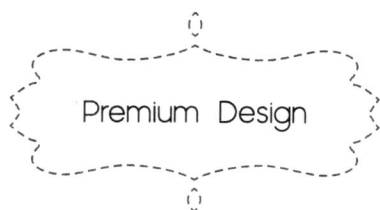

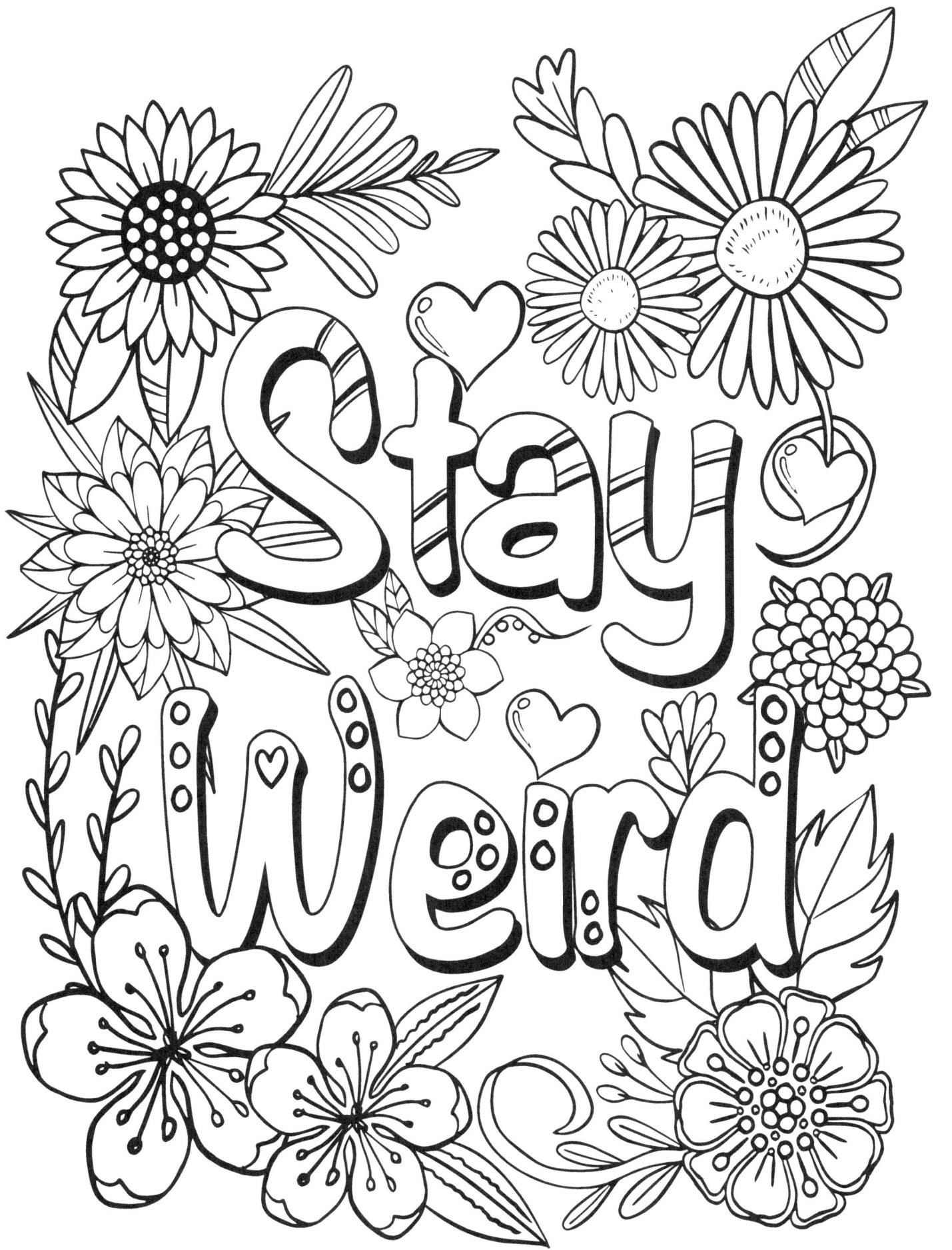

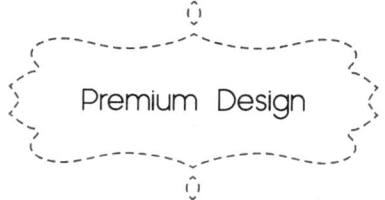

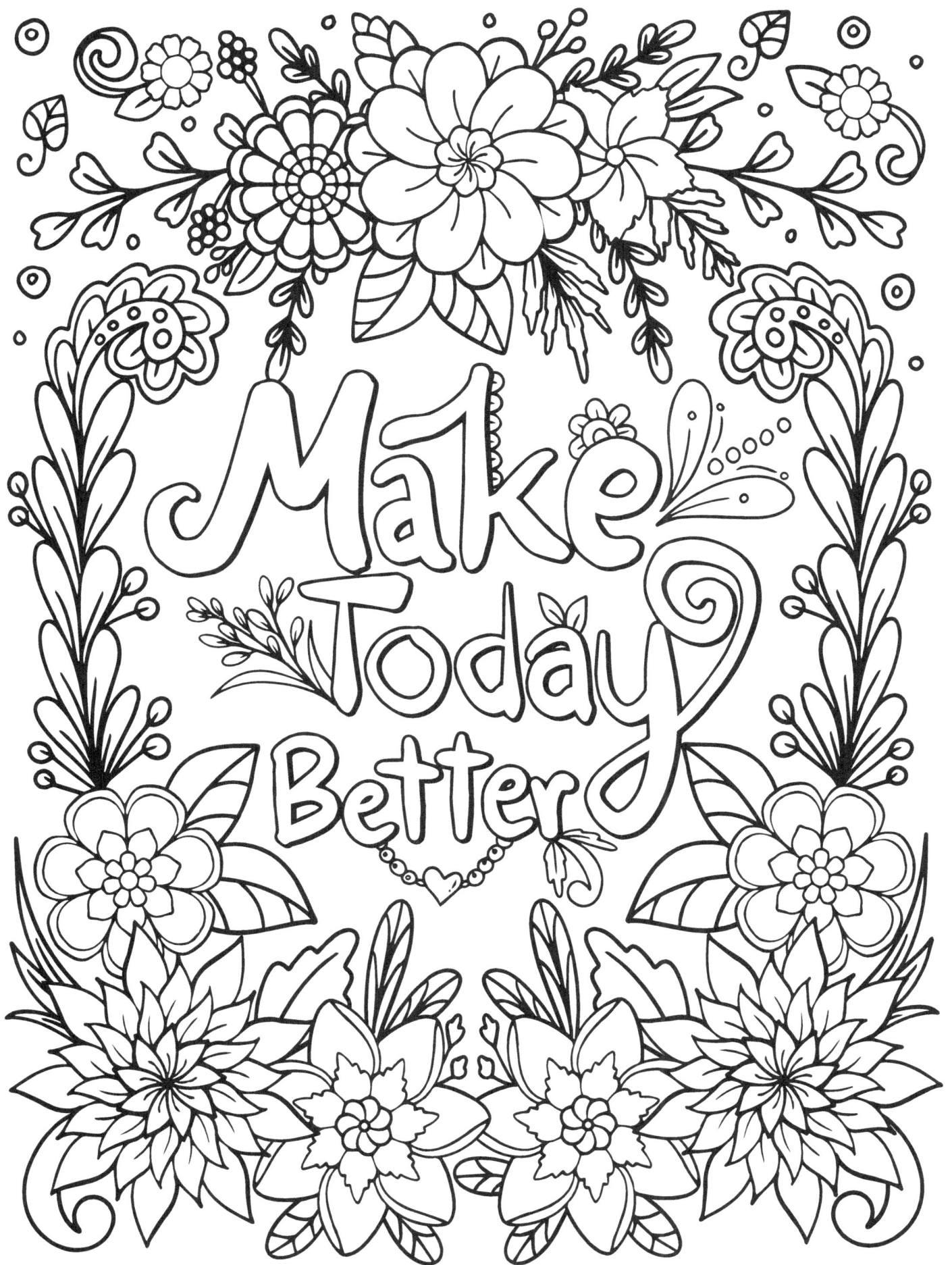

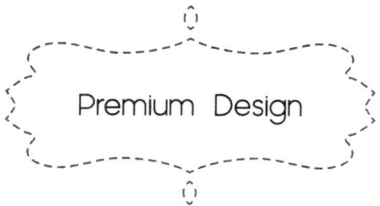
Premium Design

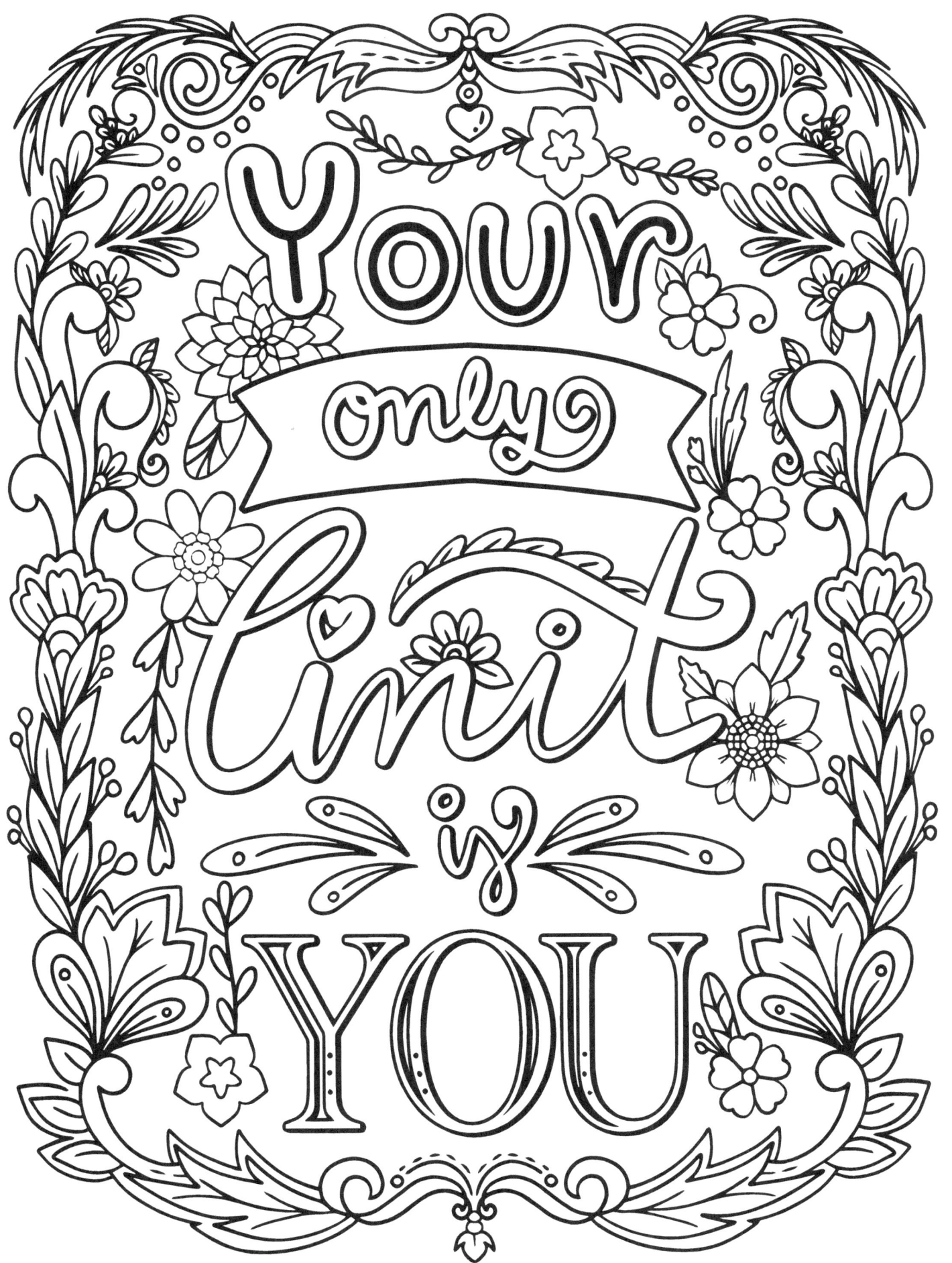

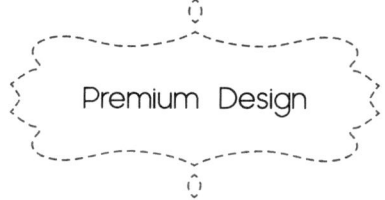

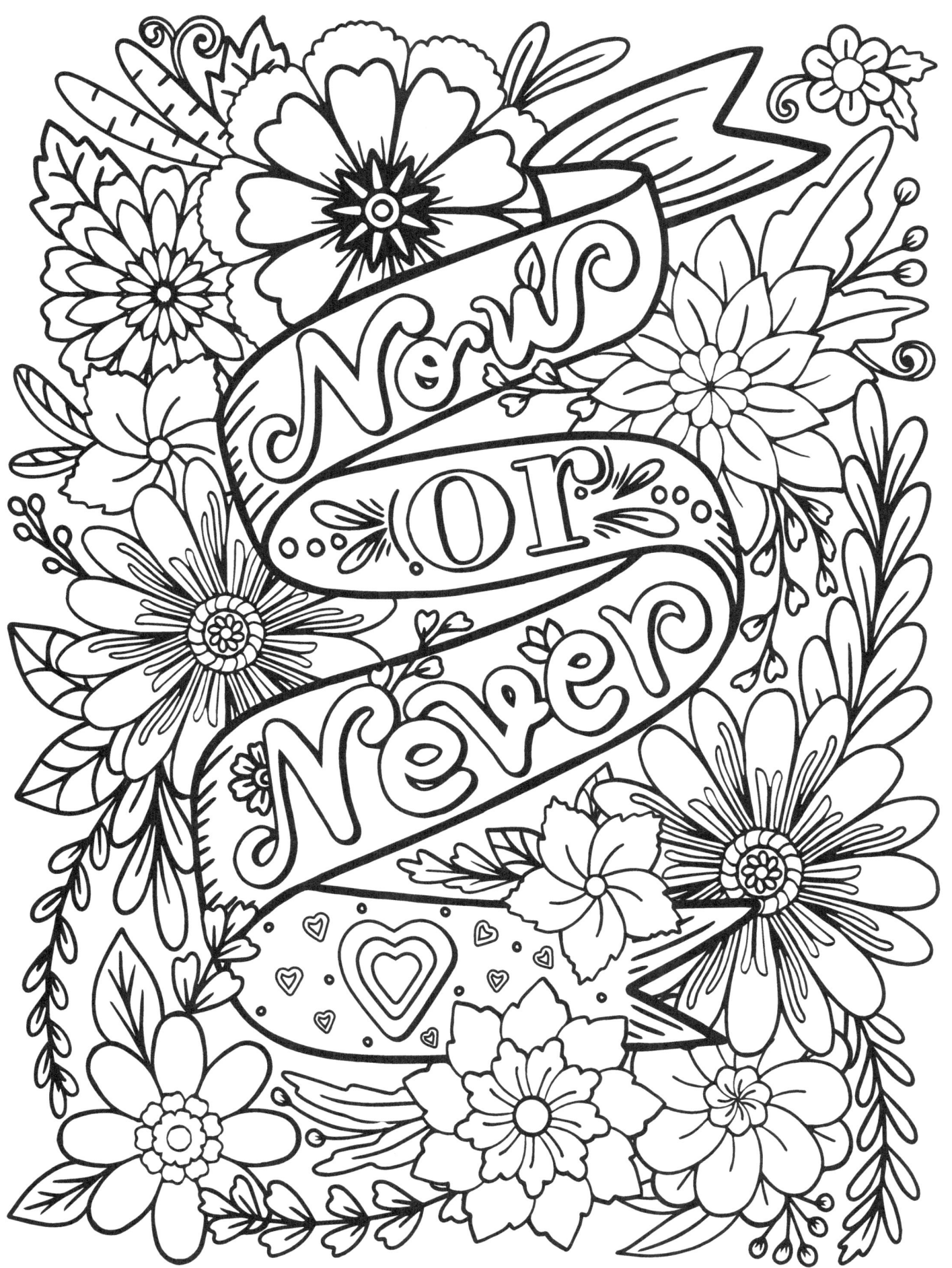

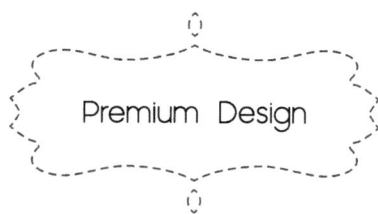

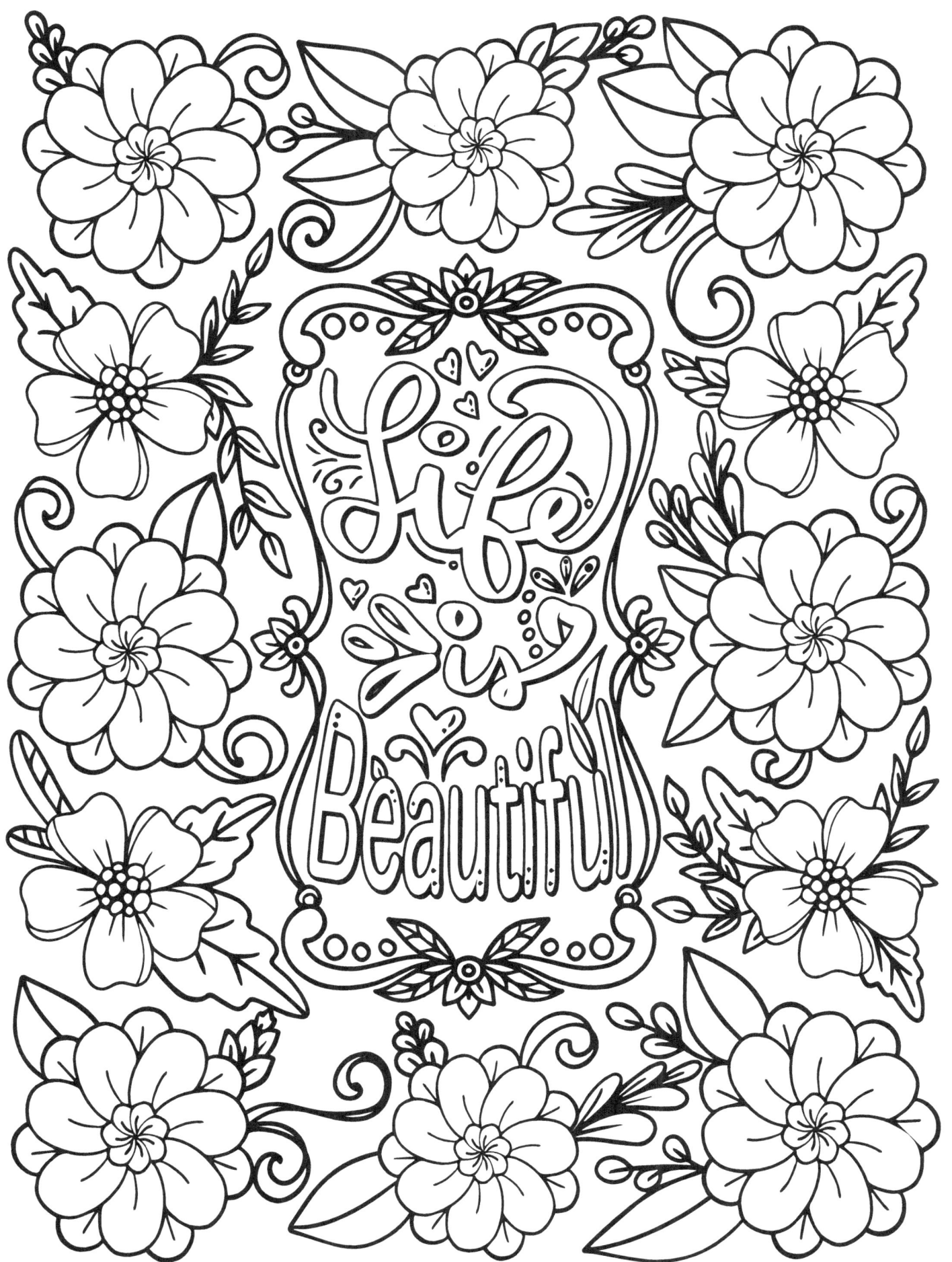

If you enjoyed this book, please leave us a review on Amazon, and check out the rest of our range at amazon.com/author/saikoprint

Thanks for coloring!